Jacob of Sarug's Homily on the Love of God towards Humanity and of the Just towards God

Texts from Christian Late Antiquity

74

Series Editor

George Anton Kiraz

TeCLA (Texts from Christian Late Antiquity) is a series presenting ancient Christian texts both in their original languages and with accompanying contemporary English translations.

Jacob of Sarug's Homily on the Love of God towards Humanity and of the Just towards God

Edited and Translated by

Dominique Sirgy

2022

Gorgias Press LLC, 954 River Road, Piscataway, NJ, 08854, USA

www.gorgiaspress.com

Copyright © 2022 by Gorgias Press LLC

All rights reserved under International and Pan-American Copyright Conventions. No part of this publication may be reproduced, stored in a retrieval system or transmitted in any form or by any means, electronic, mechanical, photocopying, recording, scanning or otherwise without the prior written permission of Gorgias Press LLC.

2022

ISBN 978-1-4632-4432-3 **ISSN 1935-6846**

Library of Congress Cataloging-in-Publication Data

A Cataloging-in-Publication Record is available at the Library of Congress.

Printed in the United States of America

TABLE OF CONTENTS

Table of Contents v
Acknowledgments vii
Introduction 1
Text and Translation 7
    Memra 63 On the Love of God towards Humanity and of
        the Just towards God 8
Bibliography 59
Index of Biblical References 61

Acknowledgments

The present homily was translated with indispensable reviews by Sebastian Brock and Fr. Saliba Er, to both of whom I am very grateful. The translation began during the first lockdown of Covid 2020, when George Kiraz sent out an announcement about the opportunity to translate Jacob of Serugh's homilies. I have deeply appreciated the chance to escape the challenge of these times amid the verses of Jacob's metrical homilies.

INTRODUCTION

> INFORMATION ON THIS HOMILY
> Homily Title: On the Love of God towards Humanity and of the Just towards God
> Source of Text: *Homiliae Selectae Mar-Jacobi Sarugensis*, edited by Paul Bedjan (Paris-Leipzig: Harrassowitz, 1907, 2nd ed. Piscataway: Gorgias Press, 2006), vol. 2, pp. 769–792. [Homily 63]
> Lines: 470

Jacob of Sarug's (d. 521) homily 63 "On the Love of God towards Humanity and of the Just towards God," chronicles the unravelling of God's love in sacred history – a common topic in the Late Ancient Syriac tradition. The homily, written in dodecasyllabic verse, builds itself around the metaphor of debt: the inability of humankind to return God's love and grace resounds throughout the pages of Jacob's work.[1] Jacob's narrative progresses from accounts in the Old Testament about sacrifice and worship and culminates in God's revelation of His love in the incarnation and crucifixion of Jesus Christ. The homily rests on the principle that God's love, revealed through His sacrifice, is unmatchable. The homily opens: "The heavens and the earth along with the angels and humanity, are insufficient to glorify you because of your love."

---

[1] For an analysis of the interventions of God's love in human life, see Mary Hansbury, "Love as an Exegetical Principle in Jacob of Serug," *The Harp* 27 (2011): 1–16.

The first part of the homily intones the theme that creation's glorification of the Lord ultimately comes from God himself. The praise of the sun's radiance, the sea's colossal waves, or the night's tranquility are all granted by the Lord. Humankind also remains beholden to God and the righteousness of Abel, Enosh, Melchizedek and others pale beside the ineffable superabundance of God's love. Jacob's verse thus echoes the wisdom of 1 John 4:10: "And love consists in this: not that we loved God, but that He loved us and sent His Son as the atoning sacrifice for our sins."

The historical birth of Jesus Christ initiates the second part of the homily. Before the Lord's incarnation, the righteous figures of the Old Testament were celebrated on earth. When Christ came into the world, however, he inaugurated a cataclysmic shift that would change humanity's orientation towards God: "Before the Father manifested his love, they were virtuous, but from the time that he delivered his Son to the cross, he astounded them."[2] Love is at the center and summit of God's sacrifice, and the consequences for the faithful are transformative. Prior to God's revelation of His love, the faithful proved their faith through righteous acts. Following His revelation, however, the faithful enter into a new relationship with the Lord where, in astonishment and awe for His sacrifice, they are bound to glorifying Him with praises that eternally fall short of the magnanimity of God's love: "For this favor, what kind of act of righteousness, can repay the Father, for everything falls short of his repayment... From that time, the whole world was bound over to praise the Father's love with unceasing thanksgiving."[3]

Jacob's homily also relates how God's revelation of His love fulfills the Scriptures and leads to the liberation of all the faithful. Isaiah 40 prophesied the coming of the Lord and the establishment of everlasting justice: "And the glory of the Lord will be revealed, and all humanity together will see it... But those

---

[2] Lines 303–4.
[3] Lines 423–4 and 445–6.

who wait upon the Lord will renew their strength; they will mount up with wings like eagles."[4] The homily confirms the realization of this prophecy with its description of a return to the Lord following Christ's coming that heals the wounded, frees the imprisoned, and magnifies the humble. As with the rest of his homily, the exegesis is rooted in both the Old and New Testaments, where prophecy is fulfilled through references to such passages as Matthew 15:24, Luke 4:18, Luke 4:18 etc.

The theological implications for Christian life are vast. Of utmost consequence, is the possibility for Christians to win eternal life through Jesus Christ. Jacob writes: "[Jesus] died order that his beloved ones might live, for he loved them, and the evildoers saw his love by means of his death for their sake. They realized that anyone who approaches God, will live for ever with Him in the blissful light."[5] The revelation and bestowal of eternal life changes the very significance of life and death, as 2 Corinthians 5:15 explains: "And He died for all, that those who live should no longer live for themselves, but for Him who died for them and was raised again." The focus on Christ's crucifixion in the homily, therefore, is a lesson on the paramount expression of God's love in history and a statement about the monumental redefinition of the nature Christian life. As was earlier stated, the response of the believers who live this new, eternal life in Christ is to give thanks: "From that time, the whole world was bound over to praise the Father's love with unceasing thanksgiving." Here, it seems Jacob was encouraged by Psalm 148, which urges all creatures to praise the Lord and, perhaps, too, by Colossians 2:6–7: "Therefore, just as you have received Christ Jesus as Lord, continue to walk in Him … overflowing with thankfulness."

The exegesis of Jacob's 63rd homily can be read in relation to Ephrem's (d. 373) concept of divine love and human cogni-

---

[4] Isaiah 40:5, 31.
[5] Line 320.

tion.⁶ The capacity of the human intellect plays a central role in Ephrem's understanding of the human's connection with and responsibility towards the divine: Though the intellect is incapable of defining God, it is capable of understanding love and mercy. God therefore reveals himself in the human language of love and mercy through types, symbols, names and in Christ's incarnation.⁷ The latter is given priority in Jacob's homily, where God reveals Himself through love. Ephrem, like Jacob, also concluded that this love evokes humankind's praise for God.

The understanding gained through God revelation of His love also offers Christians the opportunity to participate in this love and thereby to draw closer to Him. This teaching is not so much exposited in homily 63 as it is in Jacob of Sarug's other works. In Jacob's homily "On Love" he writes that God's love led Him to grant the dead the Kingdom of Heaven through the death of His Son. He goes on further to state that God reveals His love through His Son's sufferings in order for humankind to search out God's will.⁸ For Jacob, therefore, the will of God is inexorably bound to His love: By showing His love, creatures will seek out His will, and discover that His will was to grant His creatures eternal life because of his boundless love. The text, however, is not so explicit as to claim that God's will is equal to His love, and this matter can only be determined by probing further into Jacob's greater corpus. Nevertheless, the point remains that the knowledge afforded by the discovery of God's will and, through it, His love, alights a love in human beings.

It may therefore be said that the heart of Jacob's interpretation is that God's will is for all to be granted eternal life through the realization of His love and the reciprocation that it invokes.

---

⁶ Thomas Koonammakkal, "Divine Love and Revelation in Ephrem," In *The Harp (Volume 17)*, pp. 33–44 (Gorgias Press, 2011).

⁷ E. Khalife-Hachem, "Homélie Métrique de Jacques de Saroug sur l'amour." Parole de l'Orient 1 (1970): 281–299.

⁸ Ibid., p. 286.

Jacob implies that this reciprocation is natural or involuntary by characterizing it by the language of astonishment and awe, as in the verses: "He had but one Son, whom he gave to death for all people, all wills were astonished and rose with his good will"[9] and "The Father astonished and awed them with his love, and they saw they owed him payments that cannot not be entirely repaid."[10] In both excerpts, God's love evokes astonishment in the faithful and the impulse to respond to this love. God's love therefore draws the faithful toward Him with their love, however inadequate it may be, and brings them to everlasting life.

For Jacob, love is the most appropriate response to God's love. Love surpasses the value of faith, simplicity, discernment, prayer, wonder, faith, and love – seven principal conditions in Jacob's writings for understanding God.[11] When love for God is kindled among the faithful it grants them the most profound knowledge of God. Although "knowledge," is not categorically singled out in homily 63, in particular, it may be assumed that the description of creation's increasing love for God equally implies their growing in knowledge of God.

In fact, the principle that love for God translates to the knowledge of Him is central to Jacob of Sarug's exegetical method. In his "On Elisha and on the King of Moab," Jacob writes: "And (Scripture) says to you: If you read in me carelessly, I shall be reluctant to reveal any of my wisdom to you. Either love me, open, read and see my splendors, or do not read at all; for if you do not love me, you shall not benefit."[12] Scripture only reveals its wisdom to those who read it with love. Yet it is not simply human love that guides proper exegesis but human love illuminated by divine love.[13] In this way, Jacob's understanding

---

[9] Lines 287–8.
[10] Ibid., 309–310.
[11] Mansour identified these conditions in his work: Tanios Bou Mansour, *La théologie de Jacques de Saroug*, vol. 2 (Kaslik, Liban: Université Saint-Esprit, 2000).
[12] Hansbury, "Love as an exegetical principle in Jacob of Sarug," p. 354.
[13] Ibid., p. 360.

of fruitful exegesis complements homily 63's teaching that the loving disposition of the Christian faithful is inflamed and overwhelmed by the magnitude of God's love: "All repayment offered to you, is from you, how and when can creation repay you, Lord of all?"[14]

---

[14] Lines 31–2.

Text and Translation

Memra 63

On the Love of God towards Humanity and of the Just towards God

1   My Lord, the world is inadequate to profess your grace,
       and your infinite compassion is greater than creation.
       The heavens and the earth along with the angels and humanity,
       are insufficient to glorify you because of your love.
5   When the hidden and manifest worlds profess you
       with much agitation, their requital is inadequate.
       Your good favors cannot be repaid by your creations,
       because your good will itself exceeds all repayment.
       While all creatures ceaselessly praise you,

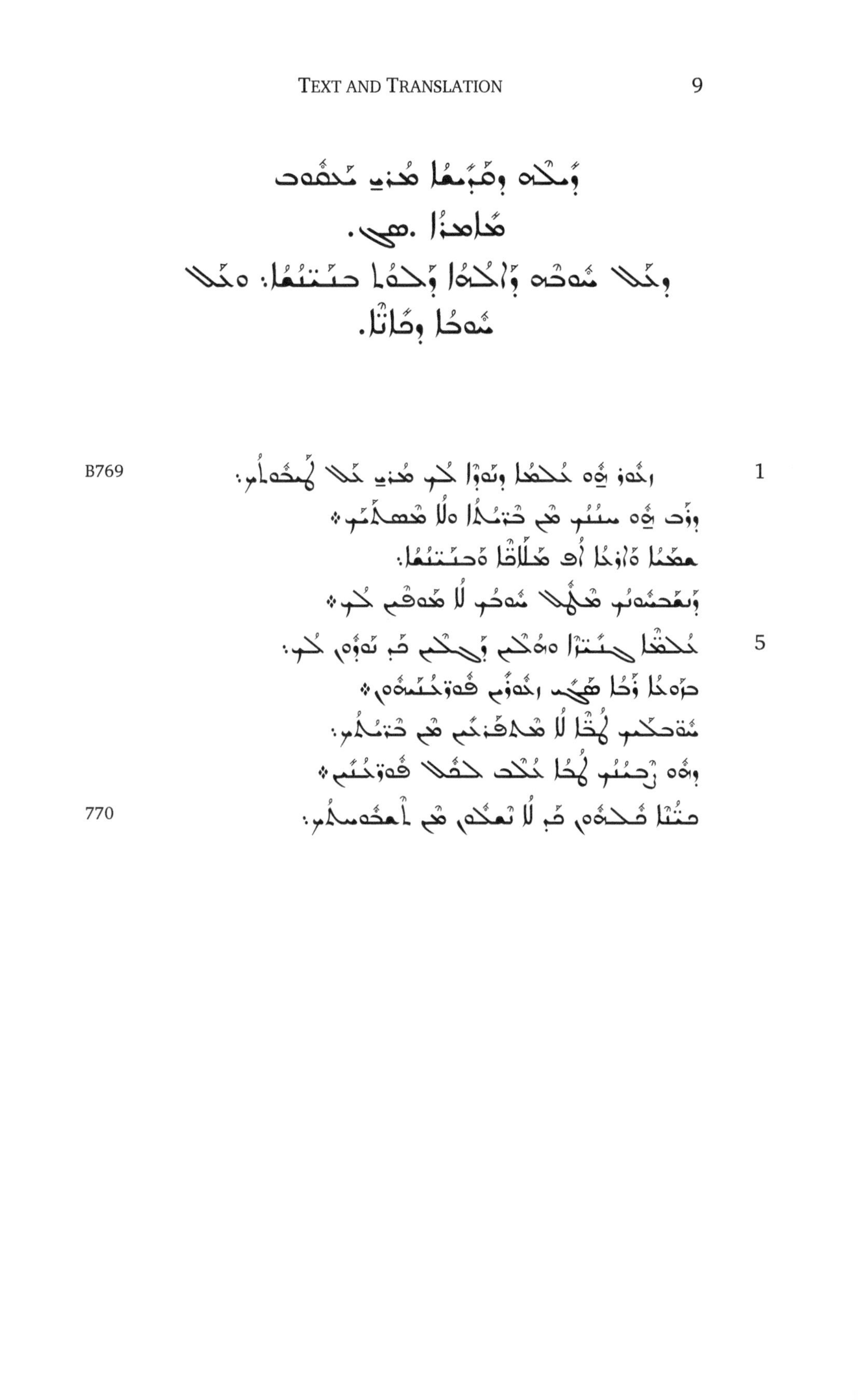

B769

	they are also indebted to you, because humankind is inadequate to repay you.
10	Whenever the angels in the heights and humanity in the depths praise you,
	the common debt still remains unpaid.
	Whenever the earth, the world, the sea, and all creation
	glorify you, they too are inadequate.
15	Gabriel's angels and the legions of Michael's angels,
	thousands of ranks and assemblies excelling in their praises.
	The assemblies of fire and the spiritual orders excelling in their shouts of joy,
	the yoked cherubim and the stirrings of the rational wheels.
	Thousands of fires and wings ablaze,
20	extended heights and all the heavenly assemblies.
	The firmament in its beauty with the luminaries arrayed in it,
	the sun in its splendor and the rays of its potency.
	The moon in its course and the stars in the array of their count,
	all the air, the blasts of the winds stirring within it.
25	The great sea and the thick fog encircling it,
	the gathered abysses and all the creeping things that dwell therein.
	The earth and its fords, and the many who populate it,
	the nations, uttermost ends, all the races and their dominions.[1]
	If all these had but one mouth,

---

[1] Cf. Psalm 148.

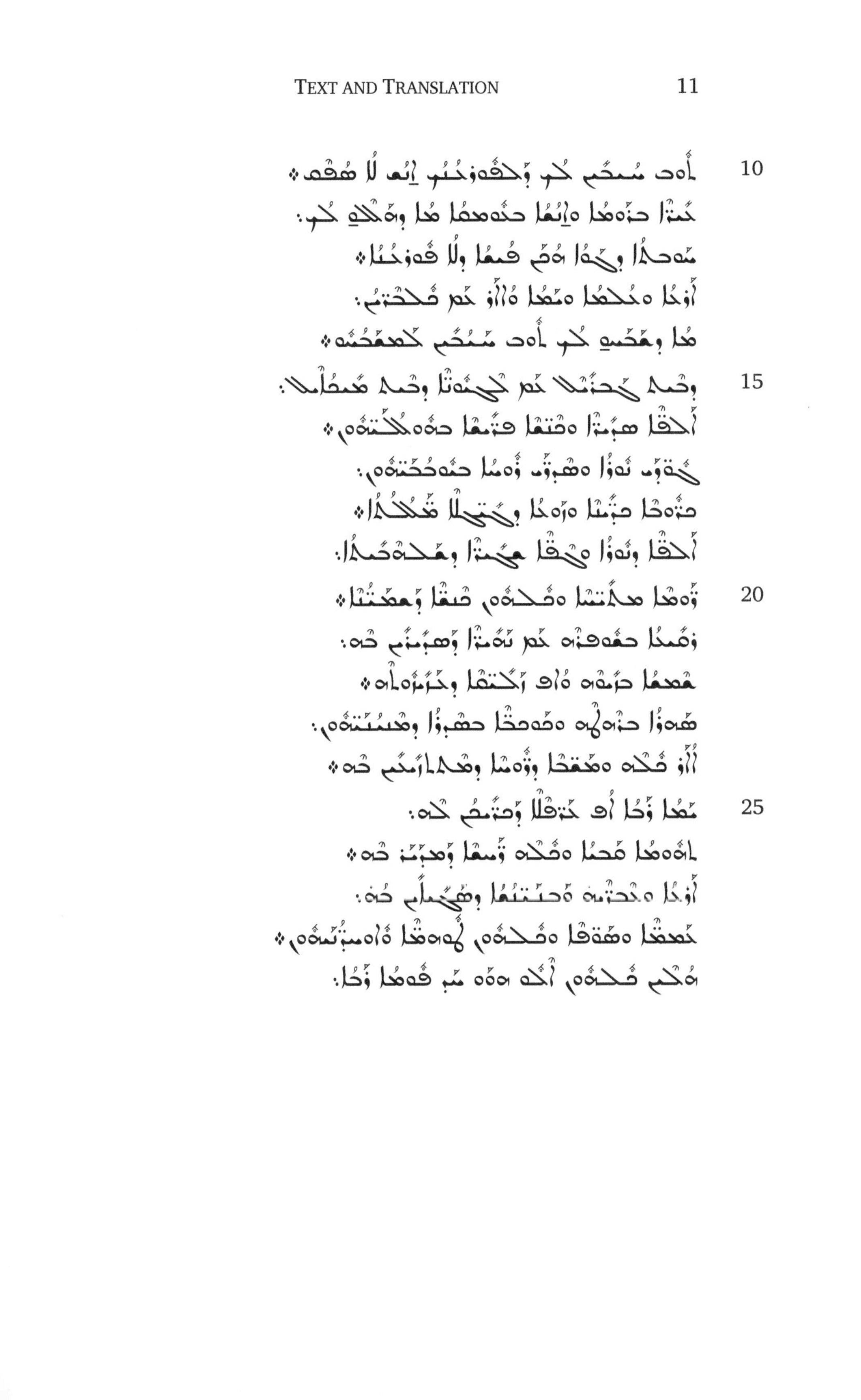

30   whose words cried glory unto you, it would not repay you.
        All repayment offered to you, is from you,
        how and when can creation repay you, Lord of all?[2]
        If the chariot, shuddering, thunders to bless you,
        its yoke is yours and it offers you glory from yourself.
35   If the seraph offers you a holy proclamation from its lips,
        its holy proclamation, its voice, and its shuddering and wings are yours.
        If the arrays of fire tremble at your glory,
        they were laid out by you and their praises are not their own.
        If the angel continually sings your praise,
40   Its mouth was so fashioned by your knowledge to glorify you.
        If Gabriel, alert, hastens to serve you,
        his swift nature and the elegance of his speed are yours.
        If Michael flies to accomplish your will,
        you granted him his flight, haste, and spiritual existence.
45   If the sun glorifies you in its path's course,
        its light, radiance and rays are yours, my Lord.
        If the moon magnifies and professes you, Illuminator of all,
        you made it bountiful in both its phases and its course.
        If the stars glorify you in their lights' course,

---

[2] Cf. 1 John 4:7.

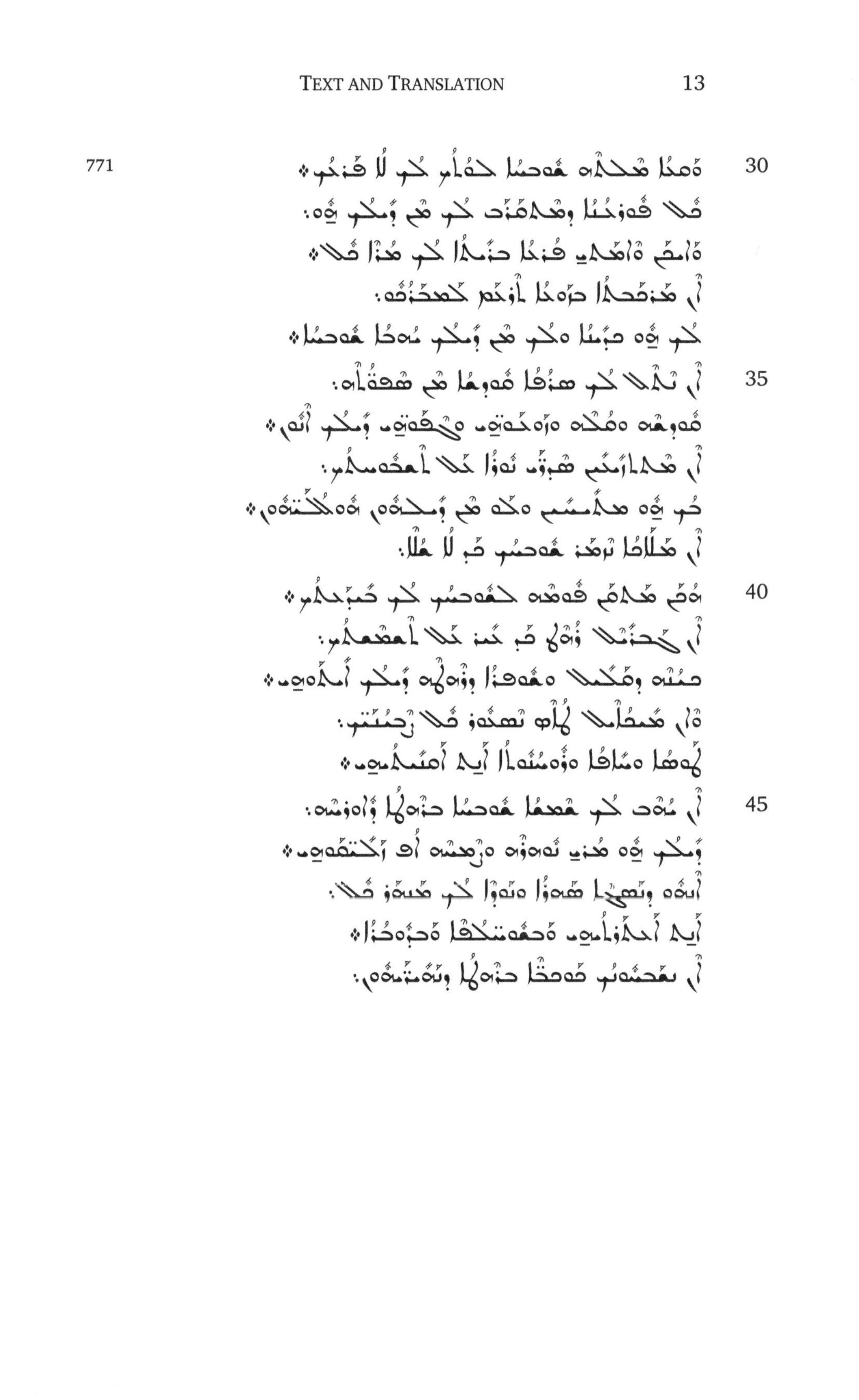

50   Their forms' ordered brightness is not theirs.
       If the sea is strengthened by its waves that sing to you,
       its immense profusion is enclosed in the hollow of your hand,
           and is not sufficient for you.
       If the abyss offers glory with the monsters,
       whatever it may possess to offer you, is from you.
55   The evenings and mornings that praise you in turn,
       the swift running of their courses is yoked to you.
       If the day lauds you with its light, Illuminator of all,
       you clothed it in a garment of light that is not its own.
       If the tranquil night professes your grace,
60   it does not offer you anything from itself.
       Whoever raises glory to you belongs to you
       and whatever he offers you is not his.
       All creatures are insufficient to repay you,
       so that they would not be able to approach your greatness without you.
65   And if all these were not able to repay you,
       then humankind is much impoverished to repay you.
       All those compensations are weak unto God,
       because humankind remains beholden to God, however much it may magnify and offer to him.
       For however long, wherever, and by whatever means he requites good favors,

772	.	50
	:	
	.	
	.	
	.	
	:	55
	.	
	:	
	.	
	.	
	.	60
	:	
	.	
	:	
	.	
	:	65
	.	
	.	
	.	
	.	

70	Adam is diligent in his repayment to God.
	The Righteous crowded, from one generation to another so that they might
	repay the good rewards of the Lord with their offerings.
	Abel chose the firstborn and fatty animal from his flock,[3]
	He purified himself, separated, and sacrificed it, in order to make an offering.
75	He honored the Lord with his whole sacrifice, which he brought to him,
	and his offering entered before the Greatness through his own blood.
	Enosh was diligent in his time as a discerning person;
	he began calling the Lord's name in order to glorify him.[4]
	He was set apart and taught the people of his age how to give praise with words
80	so that they would call the Lord's name at all times.
	His love brimmed discerningly with his Lord's love,
	and he justly offered praises at distinct times.
	He appointed the morning and evening for calling upon God's name
	in order to fasten his life to spiritual possessions.
85	He opened the earth's mouth and taught it to call
	the Lord's name every day and night.
	Enoch also persisted in elevated and divine virtues,
	refining himself with holiness and purity.[5]
	He excelled in his resplendent and pure conduct,

---

[3] Cf. Genesis 4:4, and Hebrews 11:4.
[4] Cf. Genesis 4:26.
[5] Cf. Hebrews 11:5; and Genesis 5:18–24.

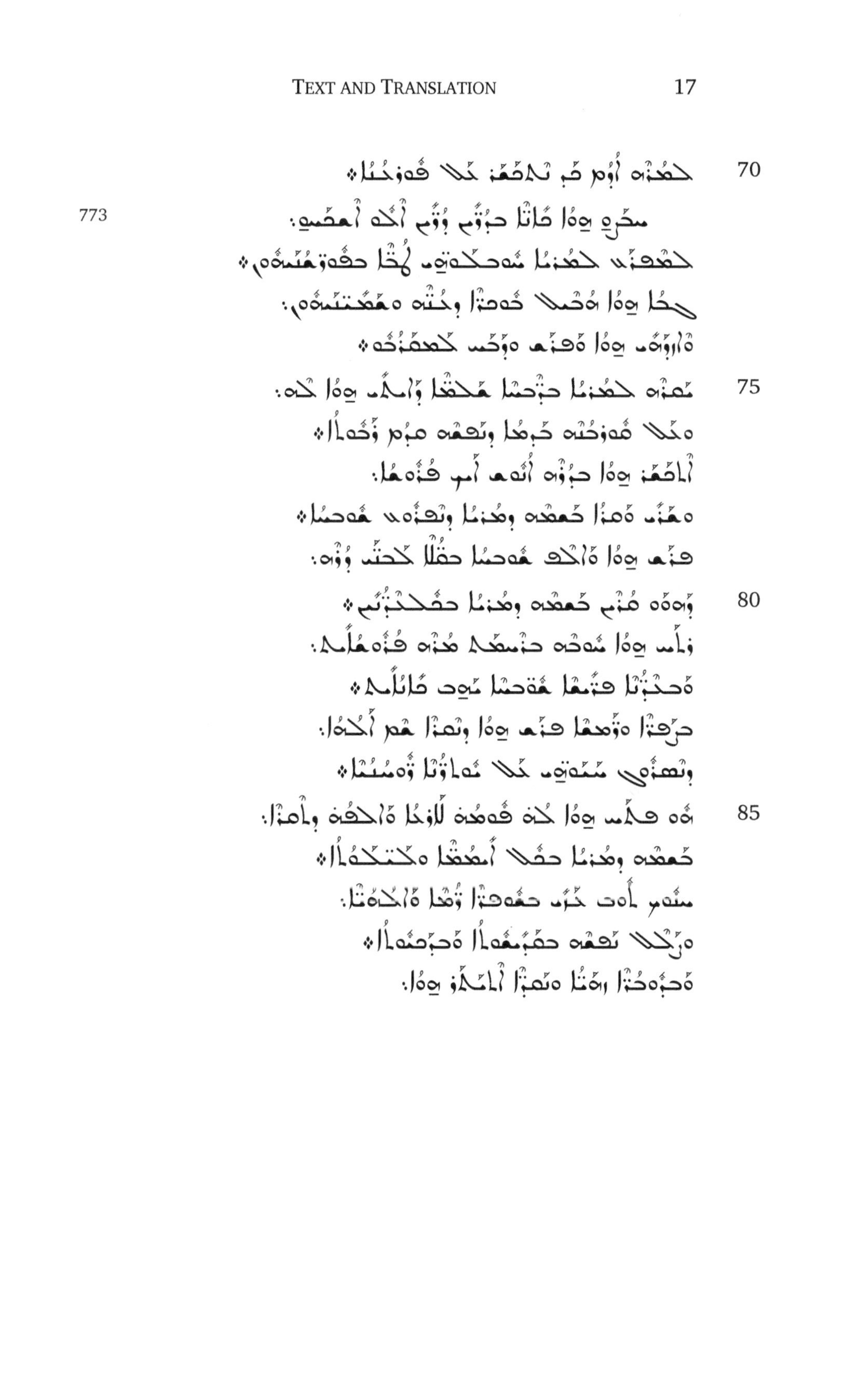

773

90   and he pleased God with his ideas that were full of love.
He grew strong through refined and cleansed thoughts,
and he lived purely without concerns or anger.
He lived without worldly impulses in creation,
And he pleased God for three-hundred years, heeding him.

95   Not in sleep or in wakefulness was any blemish ever seen in him,
nor any remiss thoughts that inclined towards the world.
Heeding the Lord every day for three hundred years,
he abided in his virtue and was not sullied by faults.
Noah also rose and beheld the iniquity of an evil generation,

100   and he wove a garment for righteousness in a bodily manner.[6]
He was armored in uprightness and innocence,
so that, if he encountered sin, it would not assail his body.
He saw how much his generation's fornication had increased,
so he set aside chastity to defeat it.

105   He saw how every man had corrupted his path with impure adultery,
and being shaken, the distinguished one would not even approach marriage.
He saw the [human] nature that stumbled and fell from rectitude,
and stood above it, persisting in his virginity.
For five hundred years, he turned his face from marriage

---

[6] Cf. Genesis 6, 7:1.

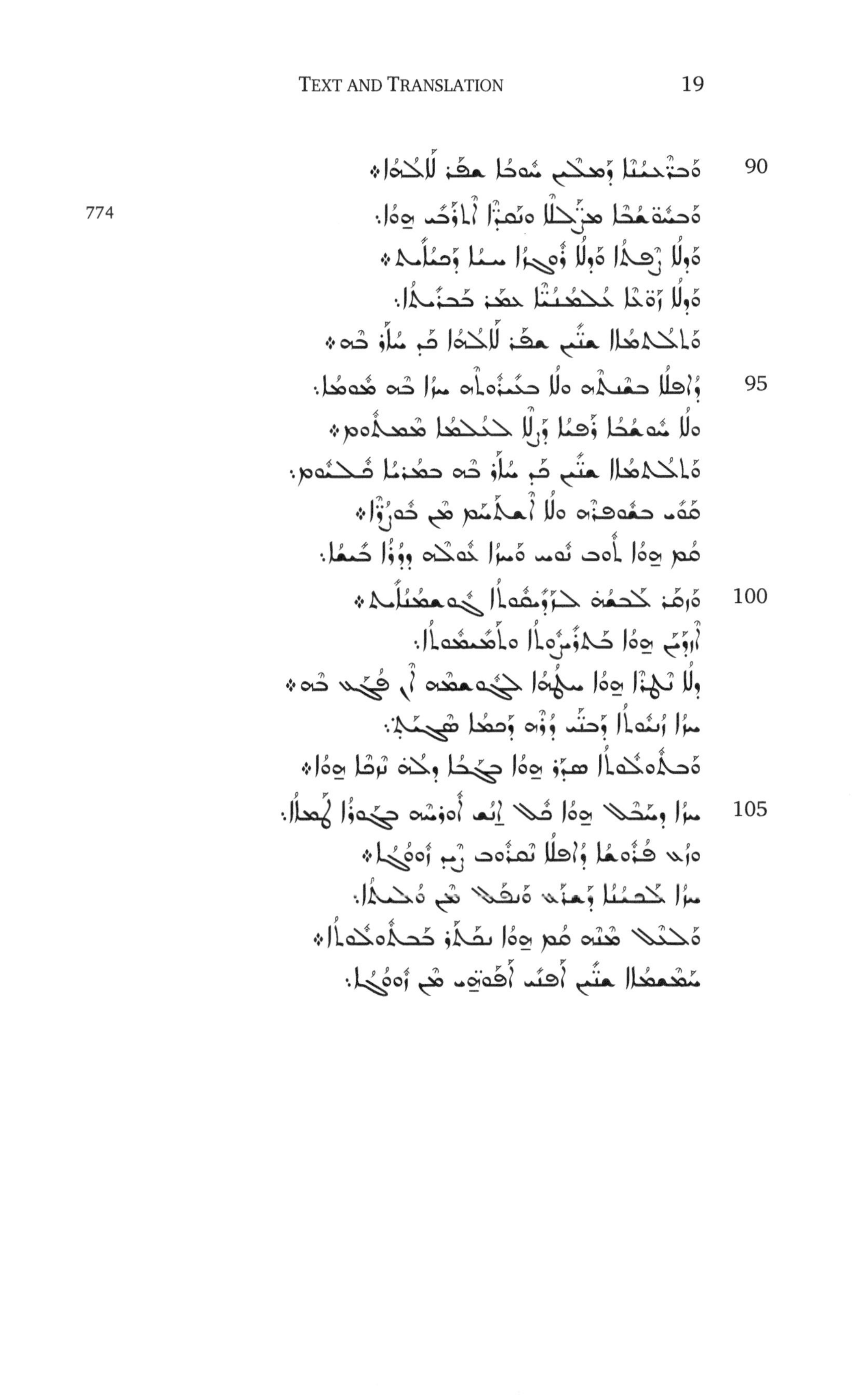

774

110   because he saw how adultery was mingled with conjugal intercourse.
He kept to his virginity for five hundred years,
and then a revelation led him to marry in order to reproduce for an opportunity.
On his own, he pleased and consoled the earth with his righteousness,
and after the desolation of the whole world, it was again resettled by him.

115   He separated out sacrifices and supplied the altar with burnt offerings,
and he was a substitute, in his time, for the world that had been consumed.
Melchizedek then rose and was filled with spiritual virtue,
a great priest and king of all righteousness.[7]
Instead of animals, he sacrificed his ideas before the great One,

120   and instead of burnt offerings he immolated his thoughts to God.
Before God, he offered his soul spiritually,
every prayer is an undefiled sacrifice.
With a pure soul he honored the Lord with discernment,
as he was not tainted by the blood of the bodily sacrifices.

125   He offered God his vows inwardly and with love,
he secretly [offered] to the Hidden one hidden gifts that please him.
His mind was made into a great censer for the Godhead,
and the smell of the love for the Lord was rising from him instead of sweet spices.
His ephod and miter were truth and beauty,

---

[7] Cf. Genesis 14:18–19; Psalm 110:4; and Hebrews 7:1–17.

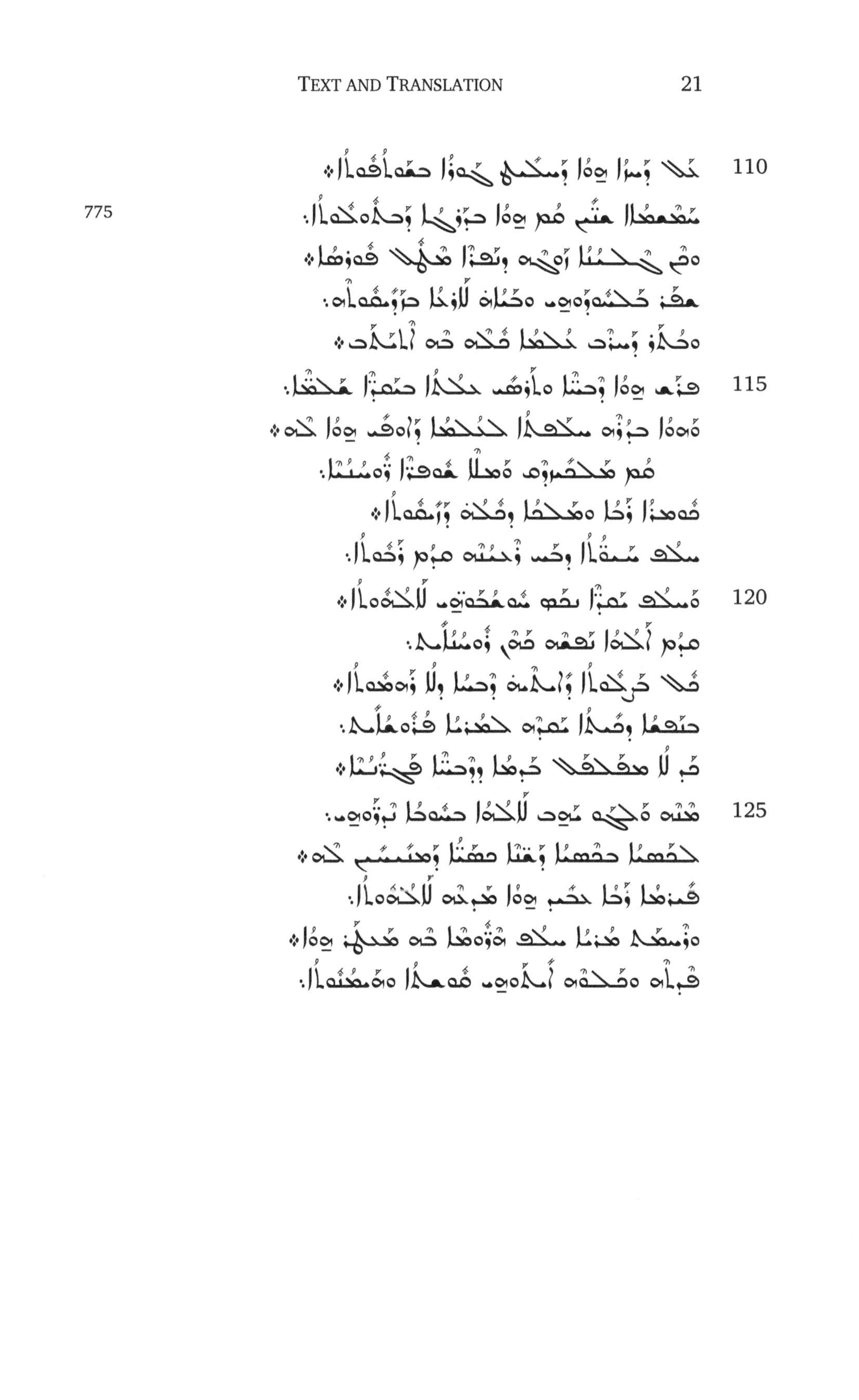

775

130   thus his garment was his mouth's unceasing praises.
      To hidden Lord, for whom sacrifices are never tasted,
      he was sacrificing every thanksgiving beloved to him.
      He knew that the Lord cannot be honored except by love,
      and with it, he was prepared in holiness to act as a priest to him.
135   The king who subjected all raging passions
      and did not struggle in any other battle.
      Abraham then rose, the friend of truth, and the good servant,
      who also established a community of faithful in his time.[8]
      He left his homeland and followed the Lord according to his call,
140   he left his people in order to draw near to God.
      He went forth as an exile and did not tire,
      for the next world was depicted before him, that he would depart to it.
      He was kindled with the love for God as though in a fire,
      and through the love of God he burned every worldly love.
145   He bound his only son to the altar as a sacrifice,
      and sharpened the blade to sacrifice the innermost affections to the Lord.[9]
      He was tried, showing with a fire and a blade,
      with whom his love lies between men and God.
      The bonds of his only son were a trial of his love,

---

[8] Cf. Genesis 25:7, 24:1, 28:4.
[9] Cf. Genesis 22:9–10.

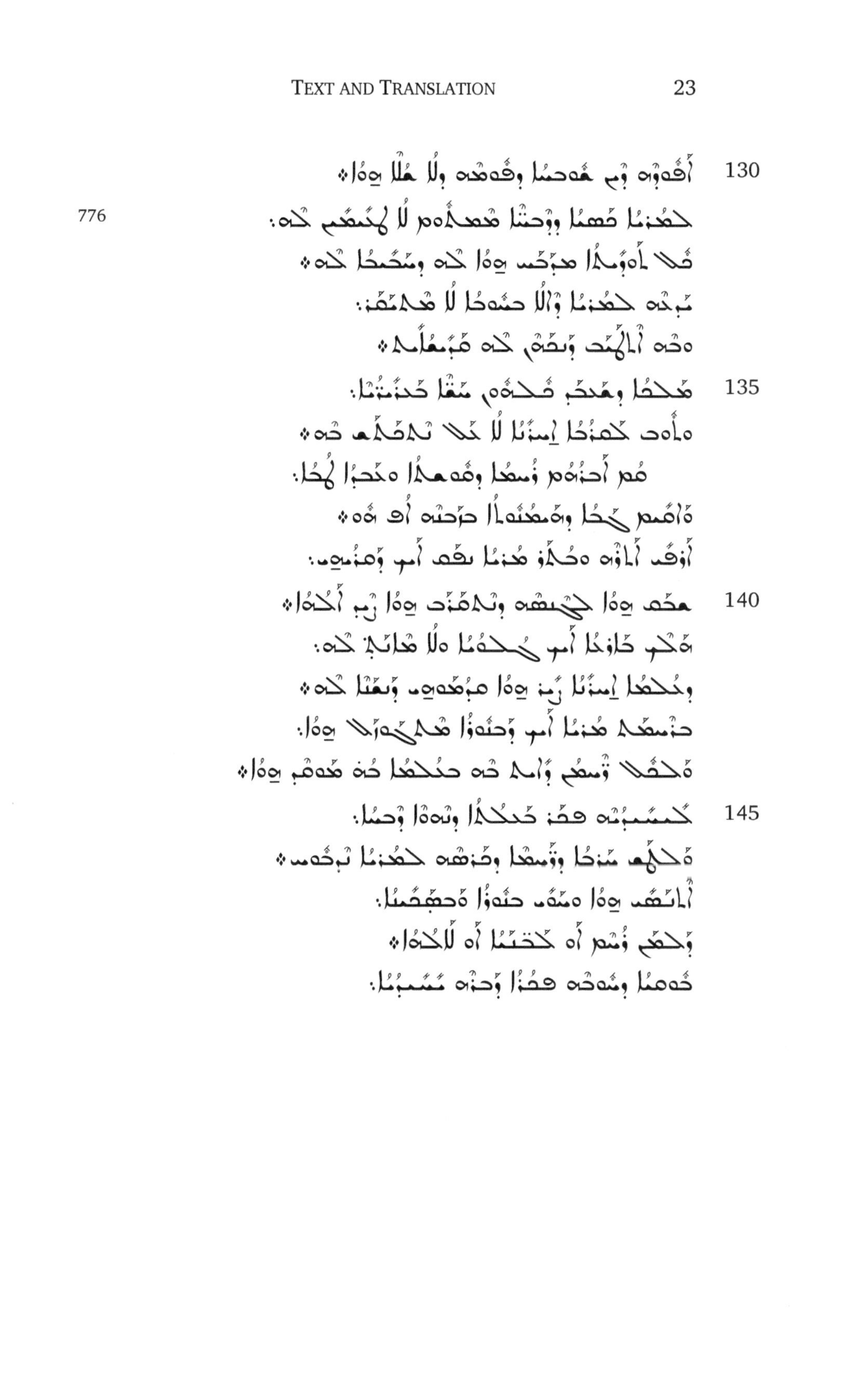

776

150   his soul's perception was an altar that he built and the fire that he lit.
His wife was taken, his land was far and his child was bound
and he did not suffer for these because he loved his Lord.
Isaac rose, who also grew in virtue
and was instructed by divine thoughts.[10]
155   His soul was filled with faith and meekness,
and he was girded with justice and rectitude.
He hated quarrels, and even at the cost of his life, he would not be provoked to anger,[11]
he loved peace and tranquility and was virtuous in deed.
Jacob also began with a righteous course,
160   and in his time, was a good laborer for faith.
He hated wealth because of the hope of what is to come,
and he left his land to gain a blessing while fleeing.[12]
Because his pure soul was worthy for a great vision,
a revelation full of wonder stirred and he was illuminated by it.[13]
165   Because he was holy enough to be a shrine for God,
the divine presence of the high One descended upon him in sanctity.
His soul was limpid, and his prayer pure and full of symbols,[14]
his love was innocent, awed and fastened to God.
In his time, Job was also distinguished by faith

---

[10] Cf. Genesis 25:11, 26:2–5; and Galatians 4:28.
[11] Cf. Genesis 26:12–25.
[12] Cf. Genesis 28:1–5.
[13] Cf. Genesis 28:10–17.
[14] Cf. Genesis 32:9–12.

150	
	:
	:
155	
	:
	:
160	
	:
	:
165	:
	:
	:

777

170   and rose heroically in the contest of righteousness.[15]
        A great calamity struck him and he was valiant in his bravery,
        so that time would show his virtue through a trial of fire.[16]
        He abounded in integrity and rectitude,
        And caused the virtue of his righteousness to shine forth in the whole world.
175   He entered into battle and became renowned by it, for he was valorous,
        the depths of the ocean encompassed him, and without collapsing he triumphed.
        The forces of the adversary encircled him,
        and when he was struck he did not fall, for he was courageous.[17]
        Despite all evil's flaming arrows that pierced him,
180   he did not succumb to the many blows because he was valorous.[18]
        The virtues concealed in his soul for God
        were strengthened through visible illnesses that his body endured.[19]
        The world was unaware of his interior wealth,
        after he had been tested by poverty, everyone learnt of it.
185   Joseph also pursued a great path of righteousness,
        and he became a mirror full of virtues in the world.
        He strove against lust through his love for the Lord,
        and because his love for the Lord increased in him, desire was defeated.
        He sprinkled his love of the High One upon the fire of the youth,

---

[15] Cf. Job 1:20–22, 2:10, 12, 23, 26, 28, 40.
[16] Cf. Job 17.
[17] Cf. Job 1:13–19.
[18] Cf. Job 27:1–6.
[19] Cf. Job 2:1–8.

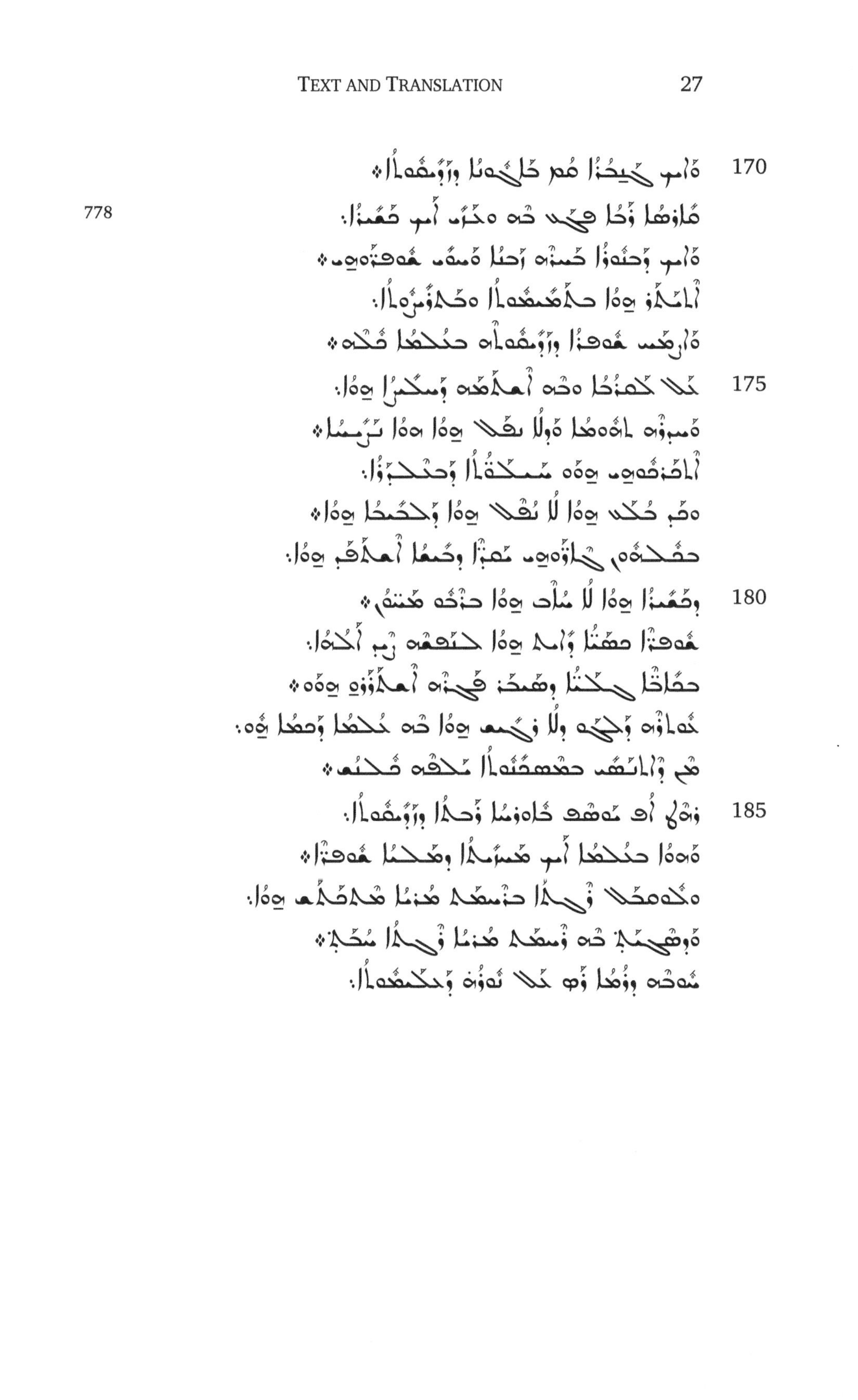

778

190 and it was extinguished from him, for he was inflamed with love.
He considered holiness a treasure full of riches,
and remained watchful that it might not be snatched from his members.
He feared adultery as one does a serpent's nest,
and fled from it so that all who become chaste might imitate him. [20]
195 He observed chastity throughout his youth with its disorderly impulses,
so that the youth might observe him and cease from their injurious ways.
He heeded God and his soul was filled with a great light,
he saw a trap and jumped, passing over it without falling in.
Moses also rose, did virtuous works with God,
200 and established a faithful group, as much as he could. [21]
He exceeded in the great virtue of meekness
and approached God through faith. [22]
He shone and was purified and shone brilliantly until he became a chosen vessel
for prophecy, so that it might be abundantly effected through him. [23]
205 He possessed deep knowledge of his soul's love for God,
until He made him like the steward for all his treasure.
He loved the Lord's people through torment and persecution,
And he lifted their disgrace and left behind all of Egypt's riches. [24]
Pinhas rose, accomplished a feat with the adulterers,

---

[20] Cf. Genesis 39:1–12.
[21] Cf. Exodus 17:2.
[22] Cf. Exodus 3:4.
[23] Cf. Exodus 34:35
[24] Cf. Exodus 12–14.

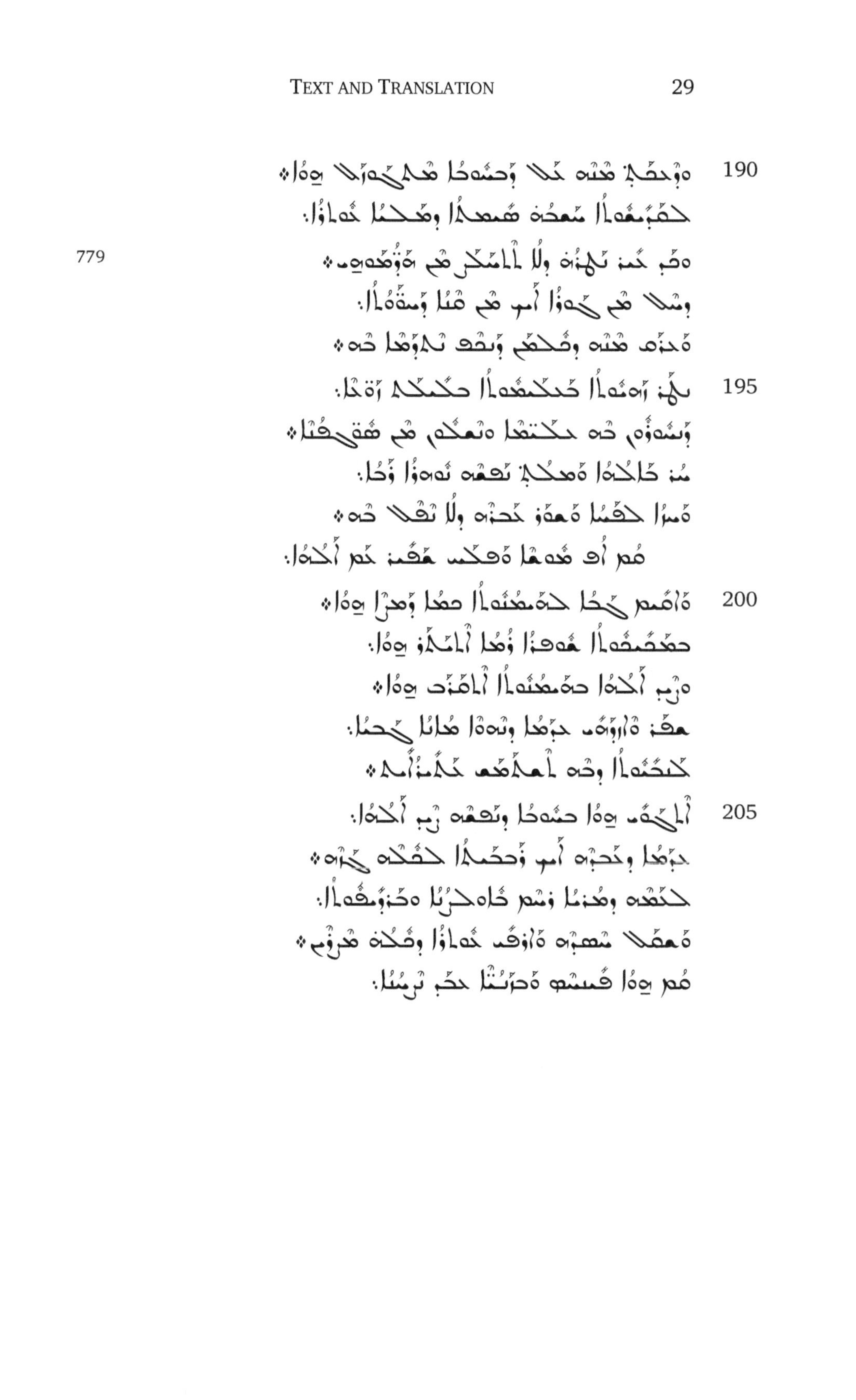

210 and his zeal showed how close it was to God.
His deed testified to how vigilant his thoughts were,
For, with his righteousness, he drove out adultery from the camp.[25]
Observe his deed and learn from him who, out his love,
took great pains to remove the evil within his nation.
215 His soul was holy, resplendent and hated adultery,
and he cast down the adulterers with his sword so that evil might cease.
He rose through prayer and hindered death from reaching many,
and after he killed two, he delivered thousands from destruction.
The just Joshua Bar Nun was also a virtuous man,
220 who was a perfect disciple to the great and resplendent One.[26]
He also desired the love of [eternal] life to be become resplendent in him,
and in perfection, thus, to approach God.
He preserved his purity by serving the tabernacle,
and for the nation, he was a second Moses with God.[27]
225 He struggled to establish the word of God in the nations,[28]
and the wonders he performed made known how lofty were his virtues.[29]
Jephthah then appeared who was also filled with faith,
Not weakening with respect to justice in the time that he served.
He sacrificed his daughter in order not to break his oath to God,[30]

---

[25] Cf. Number 25:6–12.
[26] Cf. Joshua 1:9, 5:15.
[27] Cf. Joshua 11:15.
[28] Cf. Joshua 1:10–18, Joshua 24.
[29] Cf. Joshua 3.
[30] Cf. Judges 11.

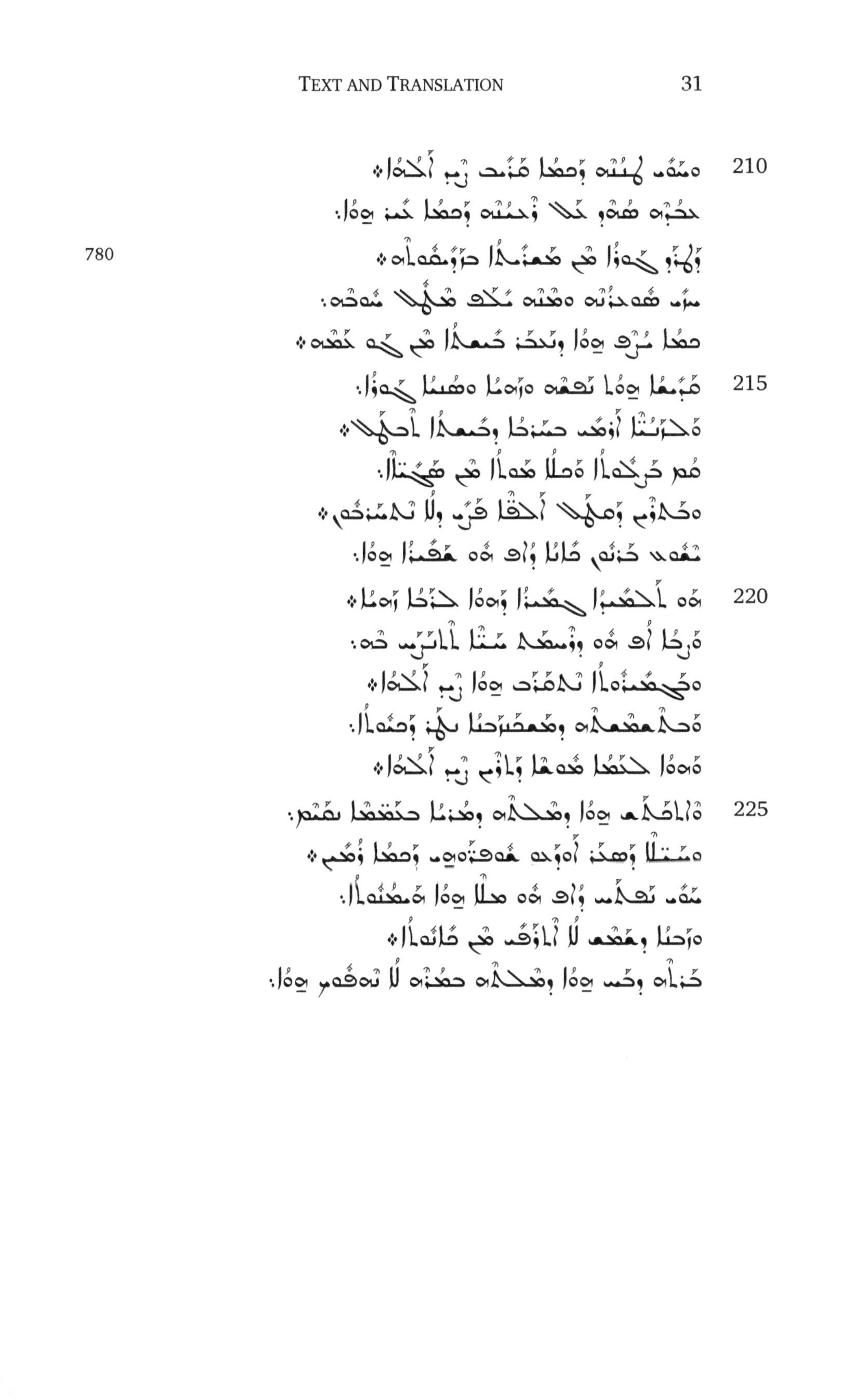

230   and behold, he is becoming and set amongst with the illustrious in righteousness.
Gideon was watchful and Barak was filled with faith,[31]
Samson was continent and Samuel pure in his prophecy.[32]
David rose and proceeded on a path of the just,
he showed himself to be without blame the moment he appeared.[33]
235   Elijah was vigilant, prepared and full of virtue,
and he persevered much in order to mingle his soul with God.[34]
He intertwined his whole life with God,
and lived in the world without worldly impulses.
He acquired a single will with God,
240   so that he and God would not become two wills.
In all the occasions that required him to fight against the nation,
he strove only to accomplish the Lord's will.
He did not desire to undertake anything from himself,
but was diligent in accomplishing all the deeds of the Lord.
245   He was alive not for himself, and not for himself was he stirred into actions,
for all the movement in his soul was in God.
Elisha also rose valiantly,
casting his path towards God in a noble course.[35]
He retained the ministry of prophecy purely,

---

[31] Cf. Judges 4–5, 6–8; and Hebrews 11:32.
[32] Cf. Judges 13–16; and 1 Samuel 3:1, 3:21.
[33] Cf. Psalm 78:72; and 1 Samuel 16:12–13.
[34] Cf. 2 Kings 1:12; 1 Kings 19:14, 17:1; and James 5:17.
[35] Cf. 1 Kings 19:19–21; 2 Kings 5:8, 2:1–21, 4:1–7 etc.

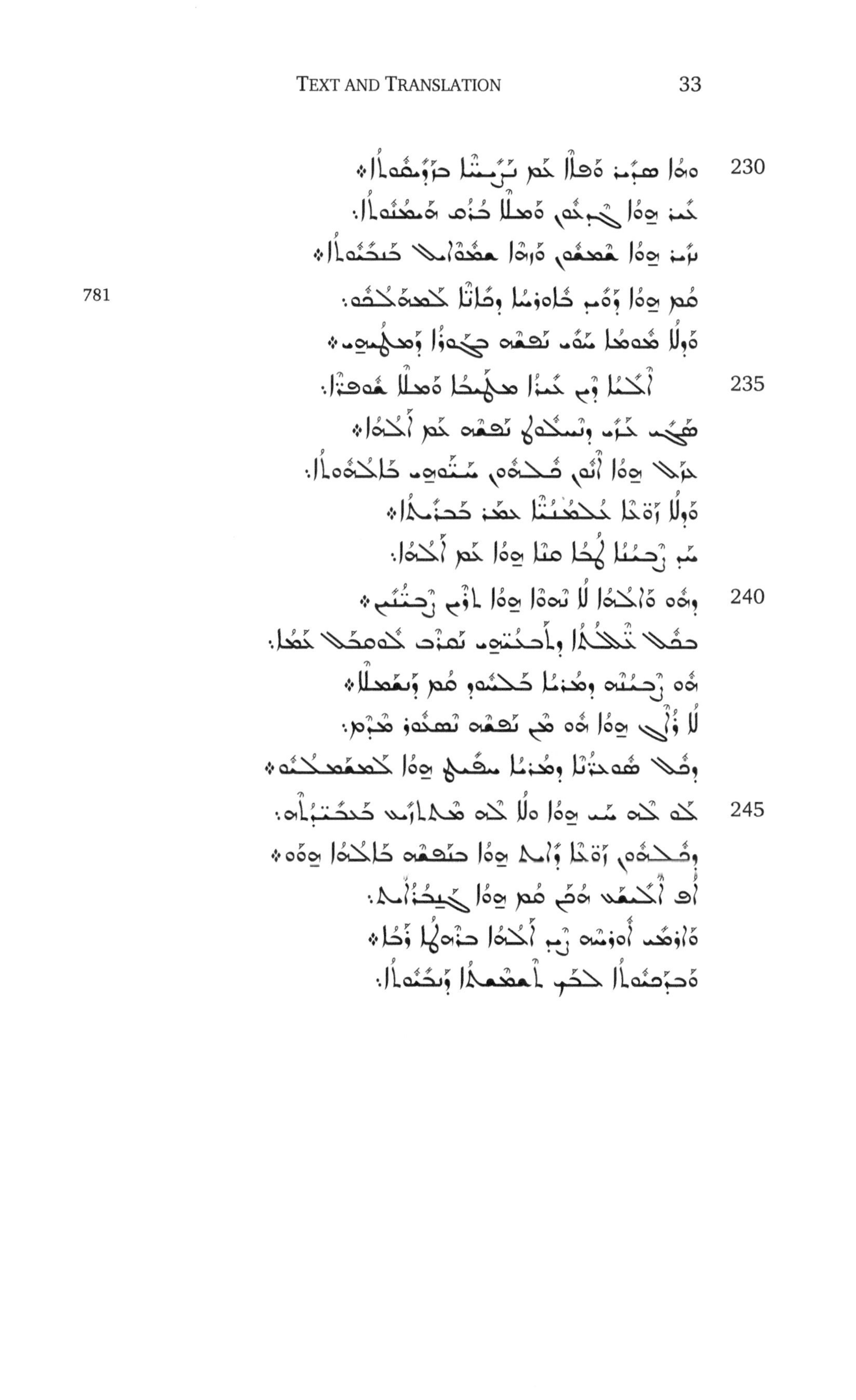

250 and practiced discipleship honorably.
He offered his soul to become the Spirit's great vessel,
and to take hold of prophecy doubly with a lucid love.
So also was Jonah who was refined by his internal love,
So that, through his excellence, there was a sign for the Son of God.[36]
255 There was also Isaiah, who prolonged his life in prophecy,
He was glorified with exalted visions through the brilliance of his soul.[37]
Jeremiah, too, purified his being from the time of his childhood,
such that the beginning of his path took its course with God.[38]
Hezekiah and Josiah with one will
260 filled with love, loved God through their conduct.[39]
Ezekiel too prophesied while being oppressed,
and pursued a path of righteousness, all the while in distress.[40]
So it was for Daniel, Ananias and Azariah
along with Mishael, who carried out good deeds for the sake of justice.[41]
265 With a great fast, and with love-filled prayer,
with self-denial and the habits of the solitaries'.
Through refinement, cleansing and purity,
and with souls full of divine thoughts.
With integrity, penitence, continence,

---

[36] Cf. Matthew 12:39; Luke 11:30; and Jonah 1:17.
[37] Cf. Isaiah 1:1, 26:9, 61:10, 25.
[38] Cf. Jeremiah 1:1–7.
[39] Cf. 2 Chronicles 29, 32:26, 34, 22:2.
[40] Cf. Ezekiel 1:2, 2:2, 24:2.
[41] Cf. Daniel 1:19.

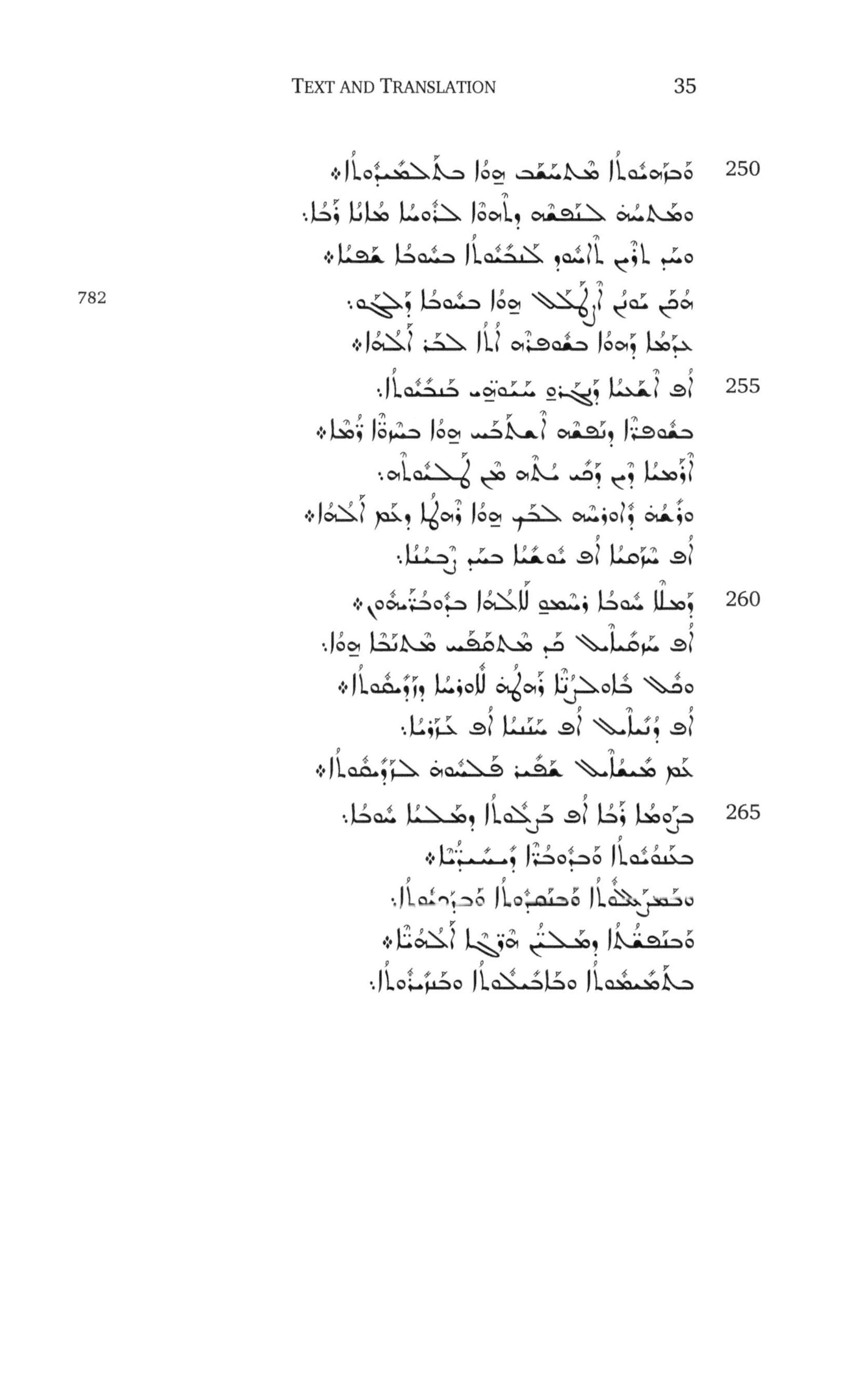

270	and all the spiritual virtues, did they conduct themselves.
	From generation unto generation, these righteous ones persevered diligently,
	And they manifested the love of their offerings to God.
	They served God with good will,
	and in their time, the world was astonished by their conduct.
275	All of creation was amazed by their deeds,
	and the world marveled at their lofty virtues.
	Their love was believed to be something great for humanity,
	and the tidings of their righteousness were precious to their generations.
	The favorable name of their character was celebrated on earth,
280	and a great marvel at their excellence filled its uttermost edges.
	Their virtues' service spread into all nations,
	and their love was much brighter than the sun upon the whole world.
	Then the Father also manifested his love to the world,
	delivering his only Son to be slaughtered for its sake.[42]
285	He bound his beloved Son to the cross for sinners,
	and his love obscured all excellence that had entered the world.[43]
	He had but one Son, whom he gave to death for all people,
	all wills were astonished and rose with his good will.
	He so magnified his love that whoever loved was ashamed

---

[42] Cf. Romans 5:8; Hebrews 2:9, etc.
[43] Cf. Ephesians 2:4–5.

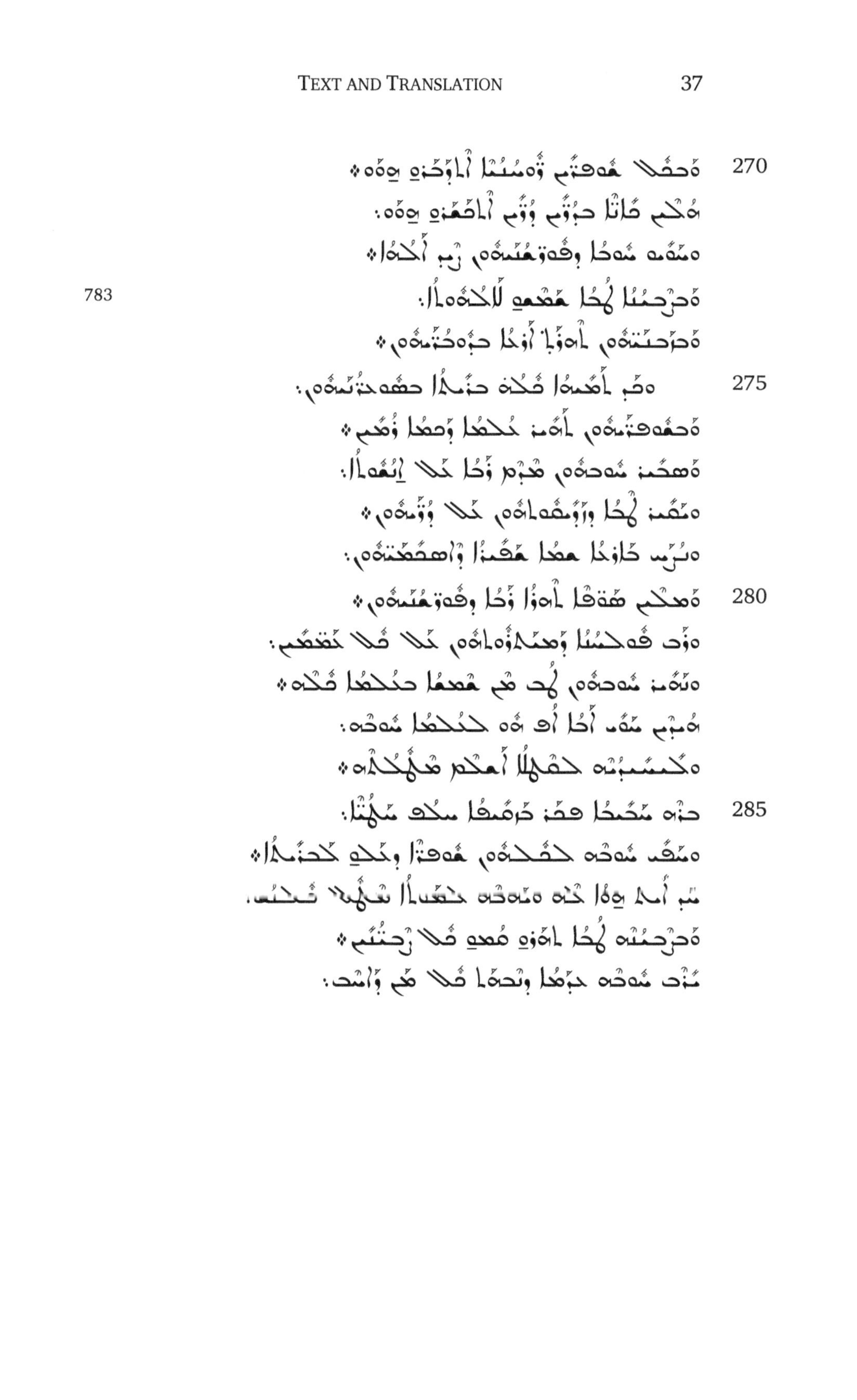

290   if he considered his love comparable to God's.[44]
      The whole course of righteousness lags behind him,
      and that excellence of all the just rose in amazement.
      He manifested his love and they manifested their love to the whole earth,
      and because God's love was gleaming, all their brilliance receded and diminished.
295   They were obscured as a lamp by the ardent sun,
      and the light of his love alone shone forth upon creation.
      The just did not attain, in their excellence,
      the goodness that the Father accomplished for the whole world.
      Against his will their virtues were as nothing,
300   and in proportion to his love their righteousness was unequally matched.
      His immense and good love overwhelmed their offerings,
      and beside him they were as nothing because of the rewards he imparted.[45]
      Before the Father manifested his love, they were virtuous,
      but from the time that he delivered his Son to the cross, he astounded them.
305   As they considered how much they loved and labored with him,
      they beheld his only Son suspended on the cross and shuddered from his love.[46]
      When they deemed themselves equal to his justice,
      they perceived, through his cross, how deficient they were next to his grace.
      The Father astonished and awed them with his love,

---

[44] Cf. 1 John 4:10.
[45] Cf. Romans 8:34–39.
[46] Cf. 1 John 4:19.

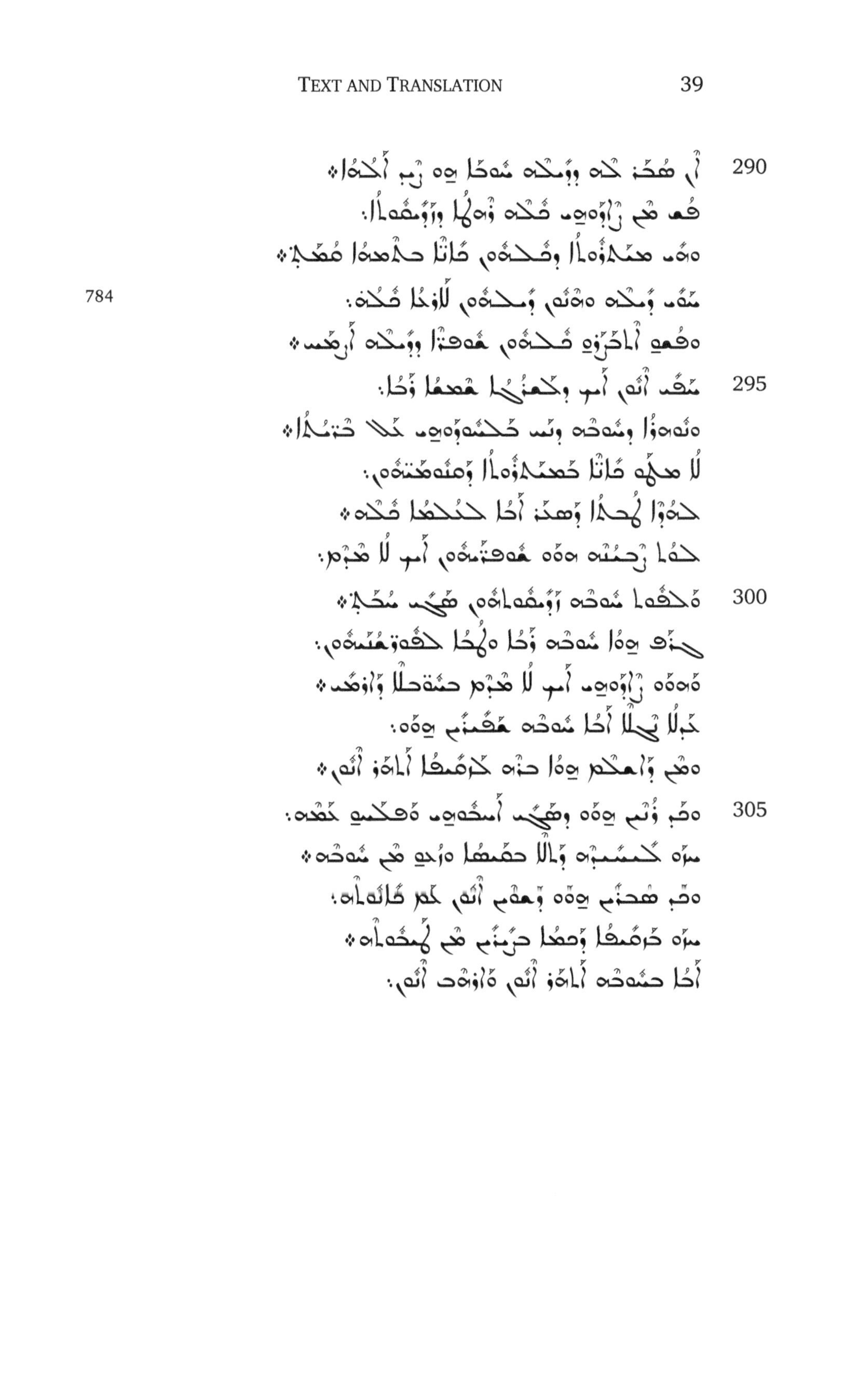

784

310 and they saw they owed him payments that cannot not be entirely repaid.
They estimated and weighed their righteousness against his love,
and they understood how lacking they were against his magnificence.
The just loved God because of God,
His (God's) [case] is greater as he delivered his Son on behalf of the wicked.[47]
315 They loved [him] because of hope in the new life,
and he loved [them] so that death might find his Son.[48]
To die in order that his beloved ones might live, for he loved them,
and the evil-doers saw his love by means of his death for their sake.
They realized that anyone who approaches God,
320 will live for ever with Him in the blissful light.[49] 320
He also knew that if he mingled with humankind,
for their sake, he would die with them to revive them.[50]
The pretext of his death was not enough to block his path,[51]
neither did humankind's evil prevent him from his salvific purpose.[52]
325 The trial of the Father's love is the death of his Son,
and henceforth, the world learned how much he loved it.[53]
The Father so loved the whole world,
that he delivered his Only-Begotten to death for its sake.[54]
Against this great love that the Father showed,

---

[47] Cf. Romans 3:5, 4:25, 5:6.
[48] Cf. 1 John 4:9.
[49] Cf. 1 John 5:11.
[50] Cf. Romans 4:25; 1 Corinthians 15:17; 2 Corinthians 5:15; and Romans 6:23, 5:21.
[51] Cf. Luke 22:42; and John 18:11.
[52] Cf. Romans 8:34.
[53] Cf. 1 John 4:10.
[54] Cf. John 3:16.

TEXT AND TRANSLATION

330 what does the righteous have to present to him?
Who [else] would have handed his Son over to the cross on behalf of sinners,
and enemies in order to give them life?
Who [else] would hand over his only Son for his servant,
who grew angry, left, and became alienated from him in his rebellion?[55]
335 Who [else] would bind the innocent One to the cross of crucifixion,
for the sake of reconciling the evil doers, although they despise him?[56]
Who [else] would forsake his Son to be insulted by the wicked
on behalf of sinners, but the Father whose love is great?[57]
Who is the precious one that was oppressed in place of the licentious
340 without complaint for our sake, but our Lord?[58]
In return for all his good favors,
who could repay a love loftier than creation?
How can the righteousness of all the just,
whenever it gazes upon Him, consider itself comparable by any means?
345 How can the just regard their virtue,
as sufficient for this great deed that astonished them?
How might they say that their righteousness is righteous,
when God hung on the cross on behalf of sinners?
What love can show itself after this one,

---

[55] Cf. Colossians 1:21–22; and Romans 5:6.
[56] Cf. Romans 5:10.
[57] Cf. Matthew 27:39; and Mark 15:29.
[58] Cf. 1 Timothy 1:15; and Matthew 9:13.

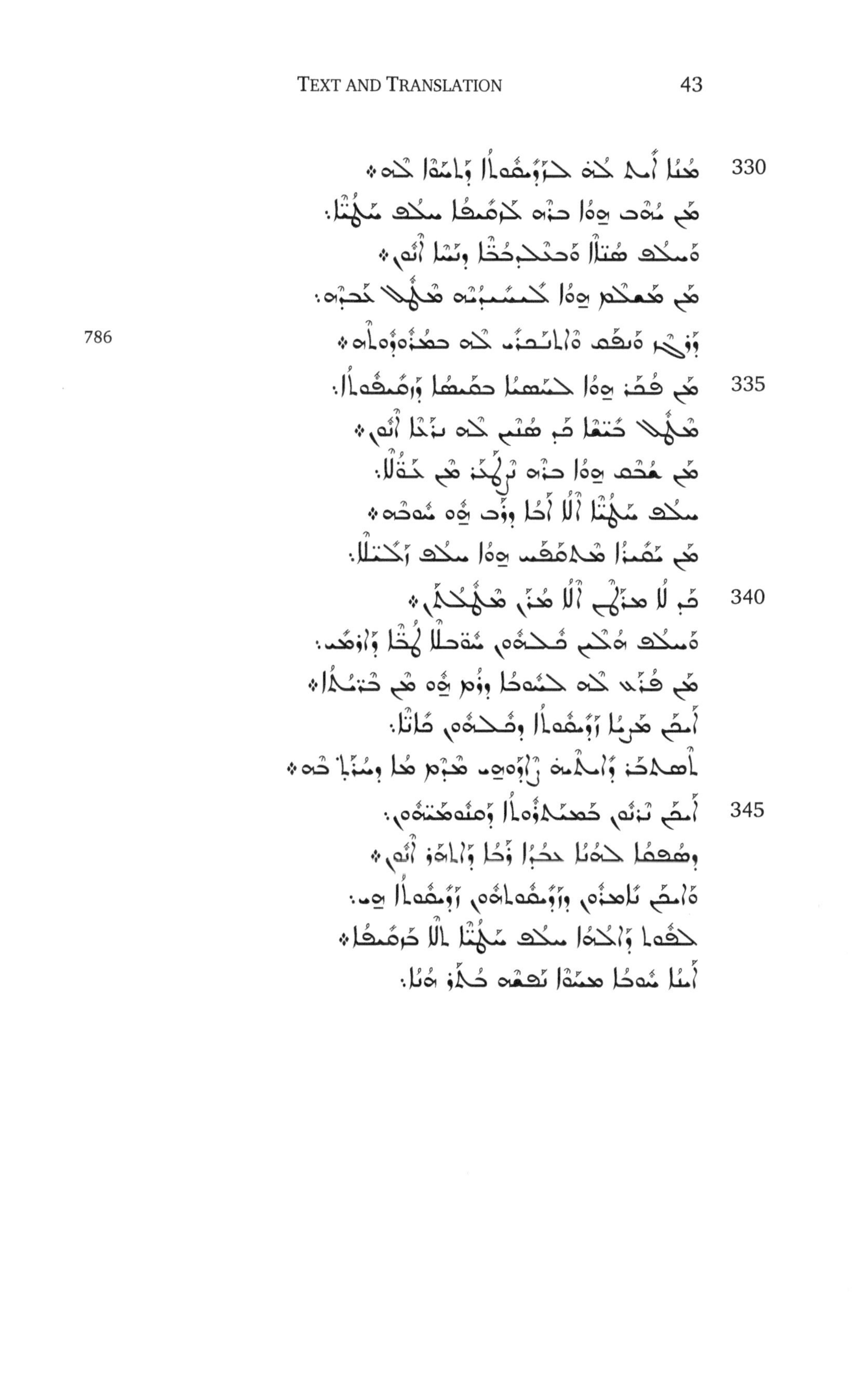

350   where the good One died for the evil doers in order to save them?
When all the virtues of their offerings are gathered,
When all the ornaments of their deeds are collected.
When their righteousness is weighed,
and all the excellence of their thoughts manifests.
355   When their virtue and deeds are estimated,
how can they measure up to the love of the Father who crucified his Son.
While they appear excellent on their own,
their love is eclipsed against that of the Father, to whom it draws near.
Let the just come to present to the magnificent One,
360   their beautiful repayments, which they set before God.
Each one will speak of his distinction,
and the earth will listen to the great honor of their triumphs.
One shows his own blood, which he poured onto his offering,
Another recounts his righteousness and rectitude.
365   One boasts how he bound his son as a sacrifice,
and his friend will reply that he wears the priesthood brilliantly.
This one states that he fled from his land for the sake of his Lord,
showing the suffering he endured for him.
There are some zealots for whom gazing upon the Lord suffices to please them,

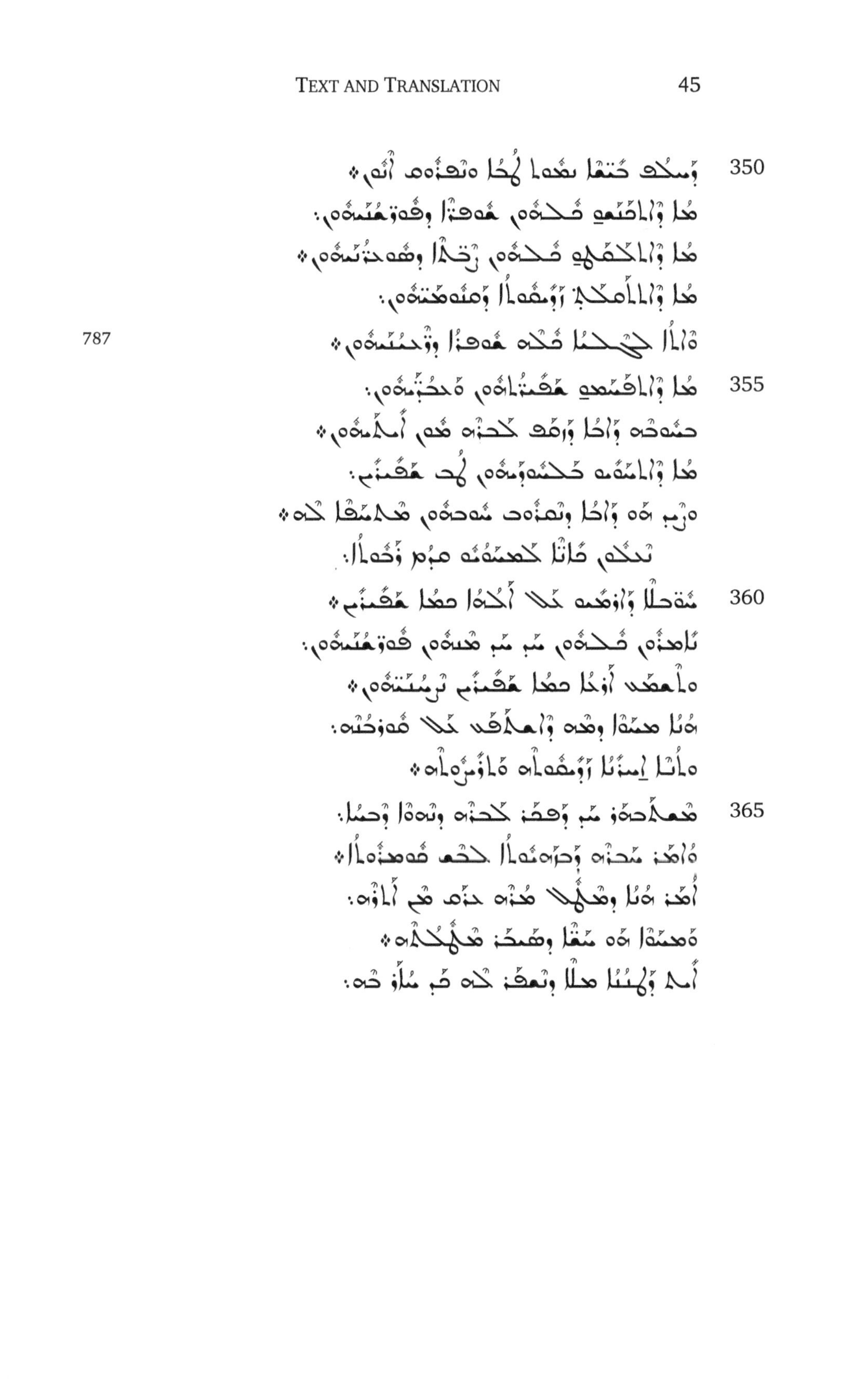

370 and still there is one who puts on righteousness that he might approach him.
One shows how he was oppressed and imprisoned because of God's love,
and another how he became meek and chaste for God's hope.
One shows how he killed his daughter for the Lord,
another, his fast, and another his love and continence.
375 One shows the excellence of his virginity and purity,
and another describes his persecution.
One is proud that he fell to lions for God's sake,
and others too, who rejoiced as they entered into fire.
One says, "I descended into the sea for your sake,"
380 and another relates the suffering he bore out of love for him.
Others show how much they were tormented for his hope,
others, with gladness, died by the sword for him.
Some were sawed in two, some wandered like animals,
others stayed in caves, destitution and misery.
385 There are some who sought him madly,
and some who, by his love, fled from inhabited lands and humanity.[59]
With all these virtues, the just will enter before God
to show him their acts and deeds.
They arrange all their labors of their ways before him,

---

[59] Cf. Hebrews 11:37.

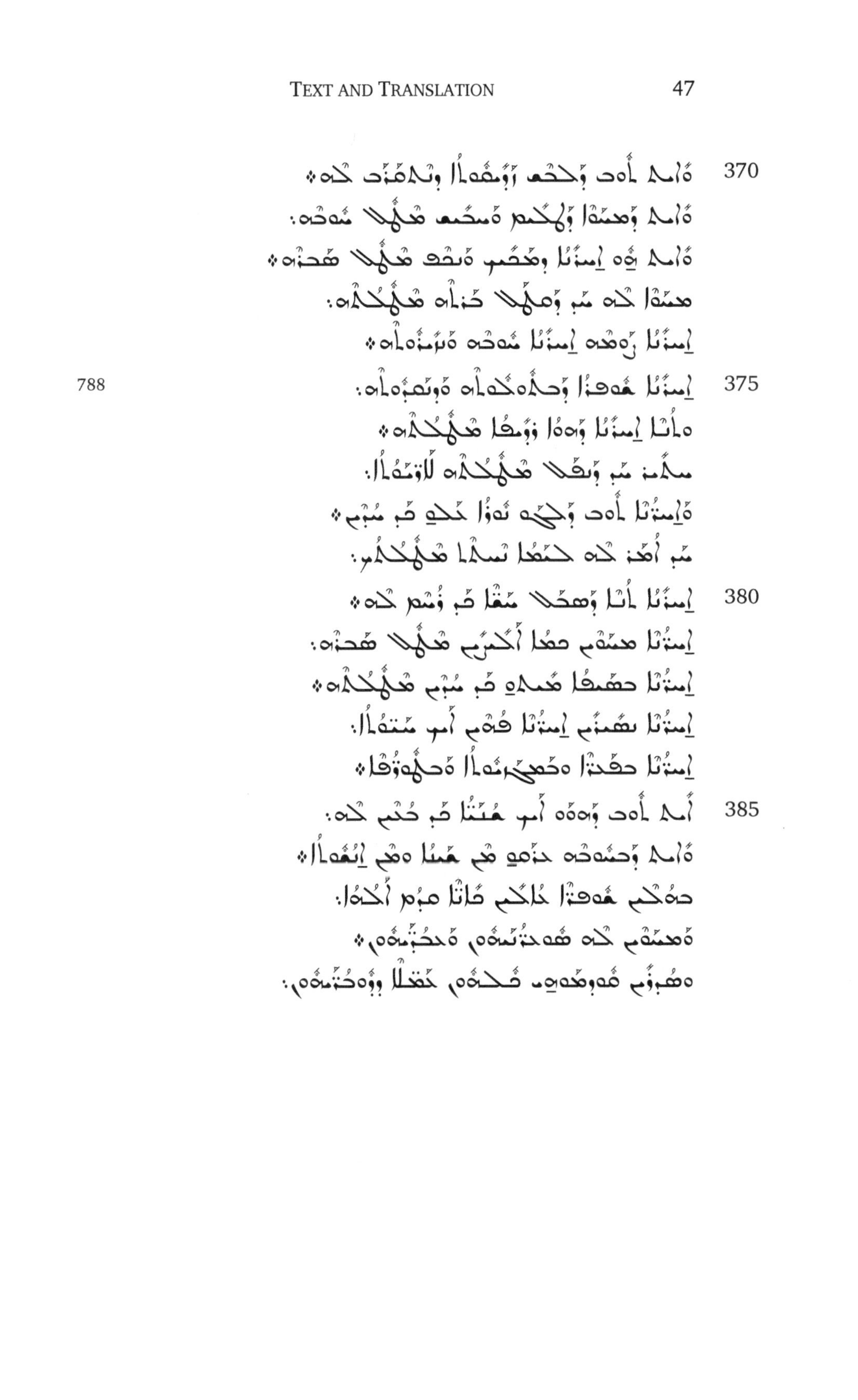

788

390   presenting him their various offerings.
Against all these virtues, the Father presents
his beloved Son, who hung on the cross for the world.
He was led to confinement, silenced in the tribunal, beaten on the head,[60]
his back was scourged, his cheeks battered and his face spat upon.[61]
395   He was bound to a column, endured blows and crucified with evil doers,
he was counted among the iniquitous, stretched upon the cross, and his hands were pierced.
He was suspended on the cross, his body was exposed, his garments distributed,[62]
and his side was riven by the lance of his crucifiers.[63]
The Father shows the world his love by means of these sufferings,
400   and astonished all creation with the magnitude of his mercy.
All the works of the righteous are inadequate,
because the world cannot compensate the Father for his Son's slaughter.[64]
He shows the nations his Son's passions, which were endured for their sake,
and the whole world is amazed because of his ineffable love.
405   And he could say, "These passions of my beloved Son
were borne because of and instead of you."
The Master of Eden accepted the spear because of Adam,
in order to open the doors which Adam had closed when he went out.[65]
For the servant, the freeman entered the land of the dead,

---

[60] Cf. Mark 14:53; Luke 22:54; John 18:12; and Matthew 26:57, 27:11–26.
[61] Cf. John 19:1; and Matthew 26:67, 27:26
[62] Cf. John 19:18; and John 19:23.
[63] Cf. John 19:34.
[64] Cf. Romans 3:20–24.
[65] Cf. Romans 5:21; and 1 Corinthians 15:22.

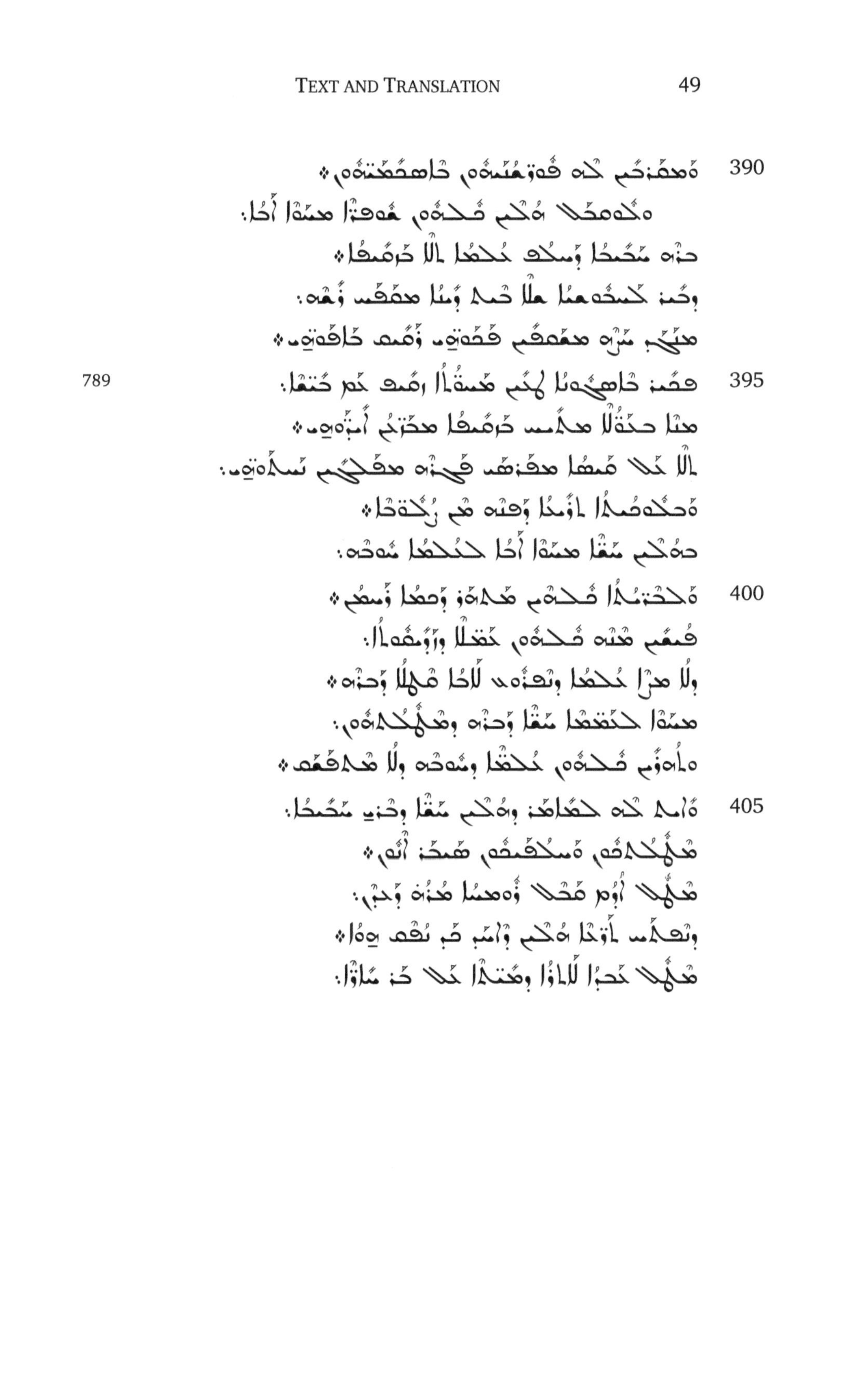

410 to loosen the fetters and bonds from him and release him.[66]
Because Adam wished to sin, my Son was insulted,
and because it pleased Adam to scorn the commandment, my Son was scourged.[67]
All those passions, scourges and the crucifixion
for the sake of all the evil doers, that they might live, though unwillingly.[68]
415 These are the disgrace and jeering that he endured when he was dishonored,
for Adam to regain the original honor.[69]
Who can repay the good rewards of the Father,
who, for the sake of the dead, delivered the living One to the cross.
Who is worthy of this astonishing deed,
420 for God himself mounted the cross in the place of humankind.
What ages will recount this love,
when all ages together are not enough to explain it.
For this favor, what kind of act of righteousness,
can repay the Father, for everything falls short of his repayment.
425 The image of the cross reveals the Father's love
and goodwill toward humankind.
He does not love mankind because he crucified his Son,
but because he loved us, he crucified his only Son.
His love was the reason for this great deed,

---

[66] Cf. 1 Peter 3:19, 3:17–22, 2 Peter 4:6.
[67] Cf. Genesis 3:6; John 19:1; and Matthew 27:26.
[68] Cf. Romans 4:25.
[69] Cf. Mark 14:65, 10:34; Matthew 26:67; Luke 22:63 etc.

410	.
	:
	.
	:
	.
415	:
	.
	:
	.
	:
420	.
	:
	.
	.
	.
425	:
	.
	.
	.
	.

790

430 were it not for his love he would not have bound his Son to the cross.
Love was with God first and through it he descended,
for he handed over his Son for our sake without sparing him.
He crucified him because he loved us, and delivered him because of the love within him,
if it were not for the love that accomplished those deeds, he would not have willed them.
435 The Father's love is great and everlasting,[70]
He fashioned the cross for his Son to be dishonored by it.
His love was hidden and the age did not perceive how much he loved it,
but through the cross he revealed his love luminously.
The Son's cross is an expositor of the Father's love,
440 and without it the world would remain unaware of its immensity.
Although God loved the world, his love was hidden,
until it was revealed through the death of his Only-Begotten Son.[71]
In the world a love shone that is brighter than the sun,[72]
creation marveled at the immensity of his grace.[73]
445 From that time, the whole world was bound over to praise the Father's love with unceasing thanksgiving.[74]
Let the good and the evil ones profess you my Lord because of your love,
which taught the world that it is boundless and greater than everything.
My Lord, let the just profess you by the course of their conduct,

---

[70] Cf. Jeremiah 31:3; and Psalm 25:6.
[71] Cf. Isaiah 45:15; and Psalm 44:24.
[72] Cf. Acts 26:13; Matthew 17:2; and Isaiah 30:26 etc.
[73] Cf. Romans 5:15; and Titus 2:11 etc.
[74] Cf. Colossians 2:7.

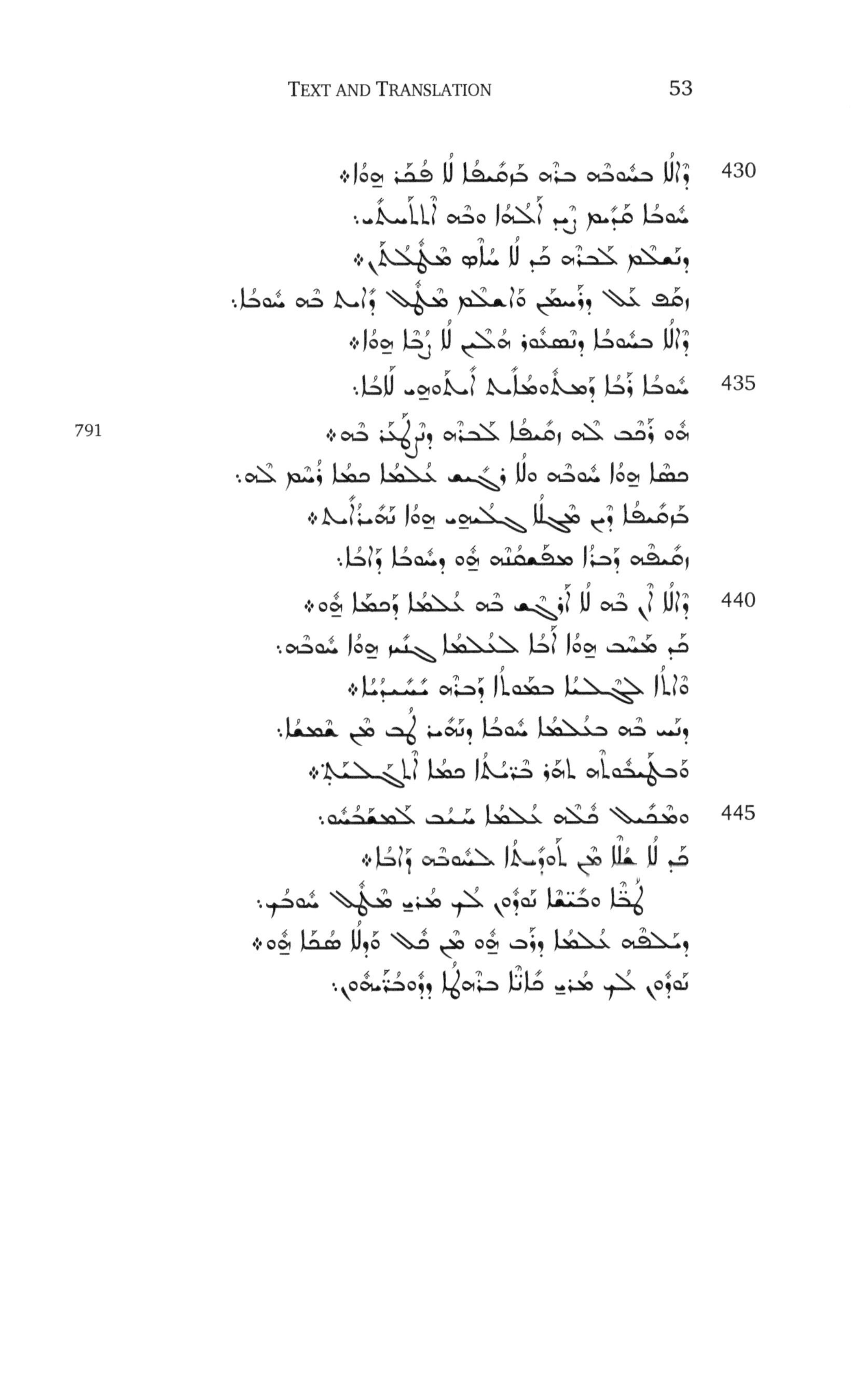

450 So, also, do righteous by the excellence of their deeds.
Let the murdered profess you by the blood that runs from their necks,
and all the persecuted by the noble sufferings of their members.[75]
Let the prophets glorify your name by the beauty of their revelations,
Let the apostles and martyrs by the immolation of their persons.[76]
455 Let the pontiffs profess you by the complete sacrifices of their ideas,
and let all priests by their dress and appearance.[77]
Let the nations and generations glorify you, my Lord, with their shouts of Hosanna,[78]
and all the uttermost ends of the earth and its four corners with their inhabitants.[79]
The sea with its waves, the abyss with its fish, and the height with its torrents,
460 the depth with its classes, the dome with its light, the earth with its children.[80]
The sky with the angels, the winds with their breeze, and the clouds with lightning,
The thunder by clamors, the mouth by speech, the mind by marvel.
Intellects by love, the cherubim by trembling, the seraphim by sanctity,[81]
the fire by fervor, wind by its force, altogether[82]

---

[75] Cf. 1 Peter 4:14,16; Philippians 1:20 etc.
[76] Cf. Acts 5:41; Isaiah 40:5; Habakkuk 2:14 etc.
[77] Cf. 1 Peter 2:5.
[78] Cf. Psalm 86:9; Daniel 7:27; Zephaniah 3:9 etc.
[79] Cf. Isaiah 11:10–12; Matthew 24:31 etc.
[80] Cf. Psalm 148.
[81] Cf. Isaiah 6:1–3; Ezekiel 10:18; Psalm 148:2 etc.
[82] Cf. Psalm 148:8–9.

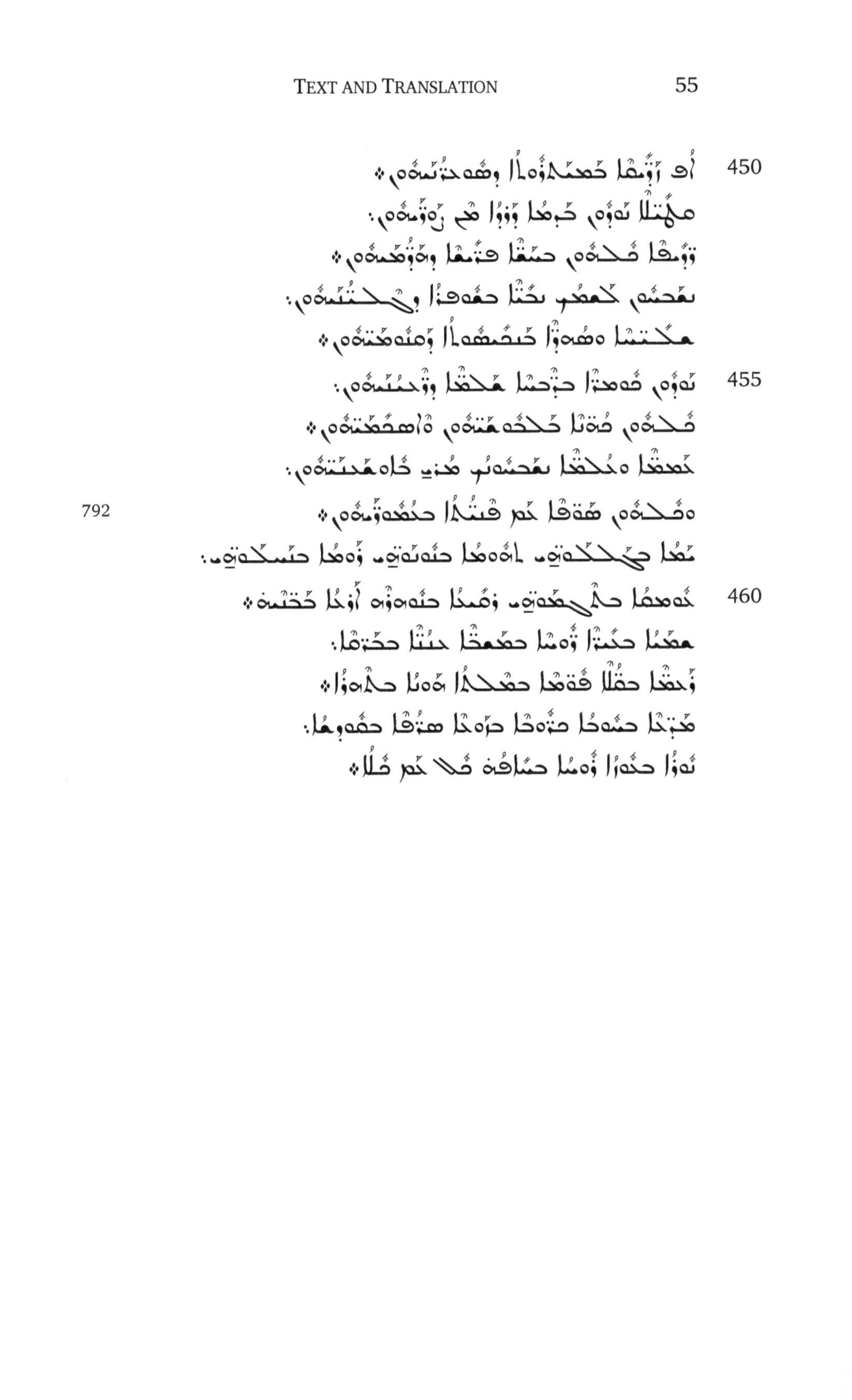

465 The scattered whom you gathered,[83] the defeated whom you established,[84] the broken whom you healed,[85]
the servants whom you freed,[86] the expelled whom you returned,[87] the little ones whom you magnified.[88]
The sick whom you visited, the ill whom you cured,[89] the captives whom you saved,[90]
the weary to whom you gave rest,[91] the angry whom you appeased,[92] the impure whom you purified.[93]
The imprisoned whom you released, the confined whom you brought out,[94] the dead to whom you gave life,[95]
470 May they profess your love, without repaying you. Praise to you.

---

[83] Cf. Matthew 15:24; and Matthew 10:6.
[84] Cf. Matthew 26:6–11; Luke 14:12–14 etc.
[85] Cf. Matthew 15:30; Psalm 34:18; Philippians 4:6 etc.
[86] Cf. 1 Corinthians 7:22; Romans 6:18; John 8:36 etc.
[87] Cf. Jeremiah 29:14; Deuteronomy 30:3; Zephaniah 3:20 etc.
[88] Cf. Matthew 25:35; Isaiah 58:7 etc.
[89] Cf. Mark 3:10, 5:29, 6:56 etc.
[90] Cf. Luke 4:18; John 8:36; Romans 6:22 etc.
[91] Cf. Matthew 11:28; Isaiah 28:12 etc.
[92] Cf. Mark 4:35–41; James 1:19–20, 4:1–2 etc.
[93] Cf. 1 John 1:7, 15:3; James 4:8 etc.
[94] Cf. 1 Peter 3:19, 4:6; Isaiah 42:7 etc.
[95] Cf. John 11:1–44; Luke 7:11–17; and Mark 5:41.

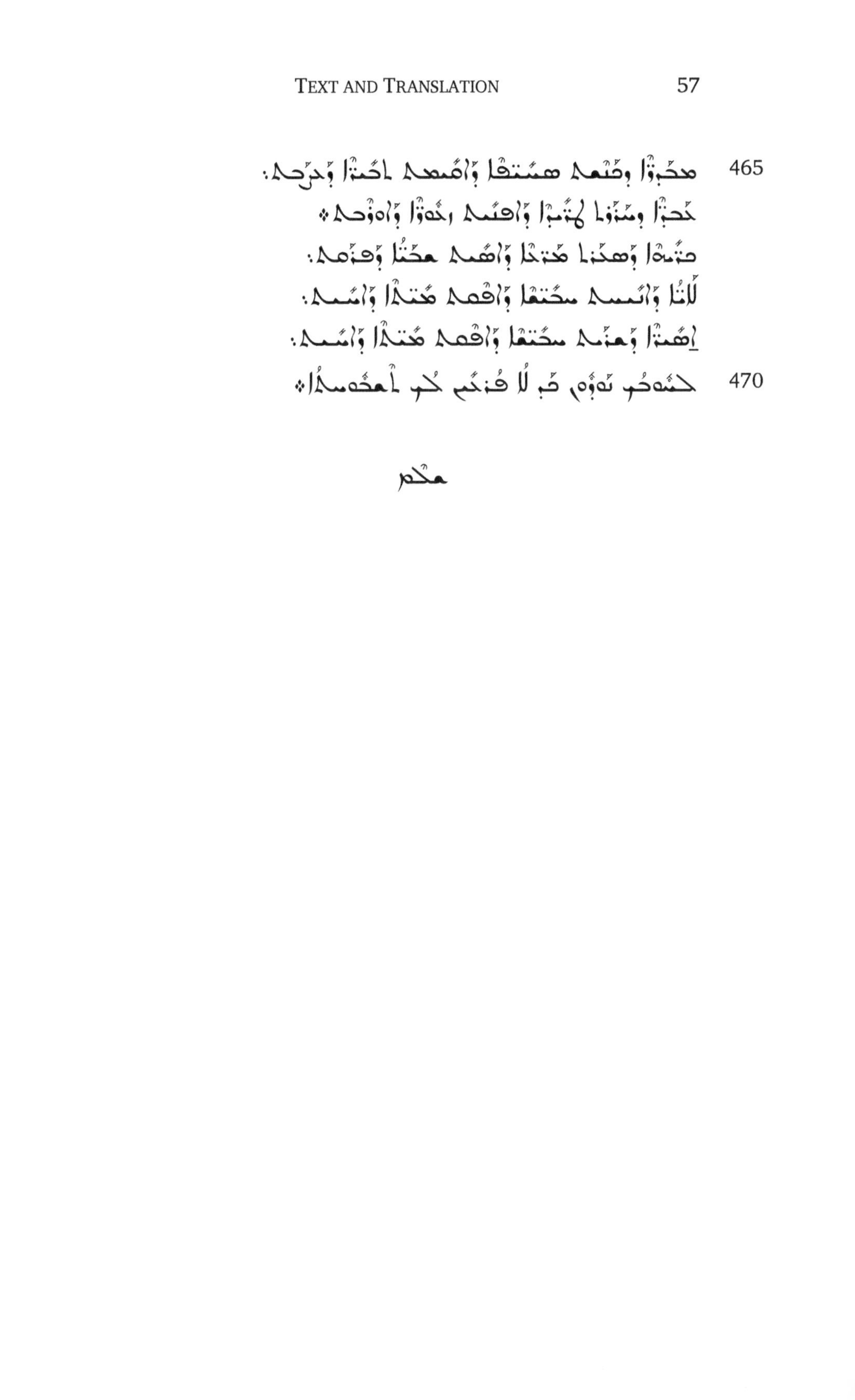

BIBLIOGRAPHY

Bou Mansour, Tanios. *La Théologie de Jacques de Saroug.* Vol. 2. Kaslik, Liban: Université Saint-Esprit, 2000.

Hansbury, Mary. "Love as an Exegetical Principle in Jacob of Serug." *The Harp* 27 (2011): 1–16.

Khalife-Hachem, E. "Homélie Métrique de Jacques de Saroug sur l'Amour." Parole de l'Orient (1970): 281–299.

Koonammakkal, Thomas. "Divine Love and Revelation in Ephrem." In *The Harp (Volume 17)*. Piscataway: Gorgias Press, 2011.

INDEX OF BIBLICAL REFERENCES

References are to line number

Genesis
  3:6   412
  4:4   73
  4:26   78
  5:18–24   88
  6   100
  7:1   100
  14:18–19   118
  22:9–10   146
  24:1   138
  25:7   138
  25:11   154
  26:2–5   154
  26:12–25   157
  28:1-5   162
  28:4   138
  28:10–17   164
  32:9–12   167
  39:1–12   194

Exodus
  3:4   202
  12–14   208
  17:2   200
  34:35   204

Numbers
  25:6–12   212

Deuteronomy
  30:3   466

Joshua
  1:9   220
  1:10–18   225
  3   226
  4–5   231
  5:15   220
  6–8   231
  11   229
  11:15   224
  24   225

Judges
  13–16   232

1 Samuel
  3:1   232
  3:21   232
  16:12–13   234

1 Kings			148:2	463
17:1	236		148:8–9	464
19:14	236			
19:19–21	248		Isaiah	
			1:1	256
2 Kings			6:1–3	463
1:12	236		11:10–12	458
2:1–21	248		25	256
4:1–7	248		26:9	256
5:8	248		28:12	468
			40:5	454
2 Chronicles			42:7	469
22:2	260		45:15	442
29	260		58:7	466
32:26	260		61:10	256
34	260		30:26	443
Job			Jeremiah	
1:13–19	178		1:1–7	258
1:20–22	170		29:14	466
Job 2:1–8	182		31:3	435
2:10	170			
2:12	170		Ezekiel	
2:23	170		1:2	262
2:26	170		2:2	262
2:28	170		24:2	262
2:40	170		10:18	463
17	172			
27:1–6	180		Daniel	
			1:19	264
Psalms			7:27	457
25:6	435			
34:18	465		Jonah	
44:24	442		1:17	254
78:72	234			
86:9	457		Habakkuk	
110:4	118		2:14	454
148	28, 460			

Zephaniah		22:63	416
3:9	457	14:12–14	465
3:20	466		
		John	
Matthew		3:16	328
9:13	340	8:36	466, 467
10:6	465	11:1–44	470
11:28	468	18:11	323
12:39	254	18:12	393
15:24	465	19:1	394, 412
15:30	465	19:18	397
17:2	443	19:23	397
24:31	458	19:34	398
25:35	466		
26:6–11	465	Acts	
27:39	338	5:41	454
27:26	394, 412	26:13	443
26:67	394, 416		
		Romans	
Mark		3:5	314
3:10	467	3:20-24	402
4:35–41	468	4:25	314, 322, 414
5:29	467		
5:41	470	5:6	314, 334
6:56	467	5:8	284
10:34	416	5:10	336
14:53	393	5:15	444
14:65	416	5:21	322, 408
15:29	338	6:18	466
26:57	393	6:22	467
27:11–26	393	6:23	322
		8:34	323
Luke		8:34–39	302
4:18	467		
7:11–17	470	1 Corinthians	
11:30	254	7:22	466
22:42	323	15:17	322
22:54	393	15:22	408

2 Corinthians		11:32	231
5:15	322	11:37	386
Galatians		James	
4:28	154	1:19–20	468
		4:1–2	468
Ephesians		4:8	468
2:4–5	286	5:17	236
Philippians		1 Peter	
1:20	452	2:5	456
4:6	465	3:17–22	410
		3:19	410, 469
Colossians		4:14,16	452
1:21–22	334		
2:7	446	2 Peter	
		4:6	410
1 Timothy			
1:15	340	1 John	
		1:7	468
Titus		15:3	468
2:11	444	4:7	32
		4:9	316
Hebrews		4:10	290, 326
2:9	284	4:19	306
7:1–17	118	5:11	320
11:4	73		
11:5	88